New Left, New Right, and the Legacy of the Sixties

New Left,
New Right,
and the
Legacy of the
SIXTIES

Paul Lyons

Temple University Press   Philadelphia

Temple University Press, Philadelphia 19122
Copyright © 1996 by Paul Lyons
All rights reserved
Published 1996
Printed in the United States of America

Text design by Erin Kirk New

Library of Congress Cataloging-in-Publication Data
Lyons, Paul, 1942–
    New Left, New Right, and the legacy of the sixties / Paul Lyons.
      p.   cm.
    Includes bibliographical references and index.
    ISBN 1-56639-477-5 (cloth : alk. paper). — ISBN 1-56639-478-3
(pbk. : alk. paper)
     1. Baby boom generation—United States.   2. United States—
Social conditions—1960–1980.   3. United States—Politics and
government—1945–1989. I. Title.
HN59.L96   1996
306′.0973—dc20
                                                    96-13397

To my sister and friend, Joan Lyons

Contents

Acknowledgments

In a less than serious but scarcely frivolous way I make the claim of teaching the longest-running course on the 1960s. In a very real sense, I have been constructing this book since that distant fall of 1971. I therefore have many folks to thank for their help in keeping me going over this quarter century.

My first thank you is to all of my students—at least *most* of them!—for their enthusiasms, for their inquisitiveness, for their willingness to ask those "dumb" questions that have often been my leads to a fresh look at the 1960s. I am not of the camp that bemoans how badly today's students pale before their baby-boom predecessors.

I must express my gratitude to the Richard Stockton College of New Jersey for providing me with a number of research grants that helped this work along. In particular, let me thank President Vera King Farris and Dean David L. Carr for their gracious support. The deepest and warmest appreciation goes out to the wonderful office staff of the Division of Social and Behavioral Sciences: the divisional administrator, Barbara R. Rosenblatt; Anne Glapion; Gail Gregson; Patricia Pruitt; Patti Williamson; and especially, for particular assistance beyond the call, Teresa Steinke. They are truly a group of people who make the office a home away from home.

My colleagues at the college have been most supportive. In particular, I want to thank those who have read parts or all of these essays: Bill Gilmore-Lehne, Stephen Dunn, Joe Rubenstein, and Laurie Greene. Others have participated in our Faculty Works-in-Progress Seminar, providing me with a forum for testing my interpretations: Dick Colby, Dave Emmons, Gholam-Reza Ghorashi, Alan Mattlage, and Ed and Jan Paul. I also wish to express appreciation to my social work colleagues for allowing me to wear several academic hats: Diana Batten, Gus Fierro, William C. Jaynes IV, Sherman Labovitz, Patricia Reid-Merritt, and John Searight.

There are three couples—colleagues and their quite extraordinary wives—who have forced me to sharpen my narrative with tender but firm, loving care, aided by exceedingly scrumptious dinners: Polly Davies and Bill Sensiba, Melaku and Roman Lakew, and Joe and Helen Walsh. They really don't know how valuable they have been to the formulation of these interpretive essays. Food for thought, indeed!

The librarians at the college have always gone out of their way to assist me. Special thanks go to Mary Ann Trail, Gail Baldwin, and Carolyn Gutierrez.

Many of the ideas in these essays began as papers presented either at the Vietnam section of the Popular Culture Association or, more recently, at the Sixties Generation conferences organized by the journal *Viet Nam Generation*. I can't say enough about the support I have received from Kali Tal, John Baky, Renny Christopher, Dan Duffy, Bill Ehrhart, Cindy Fuchs, Marc Jason Gilbert, Steve Gomes, and Ellen Pinzur. They all understand the arbitrariness of disciplinary boundaries and the all-important role of occasionally laughing at oneself in the pursuit of truth.

There are a number of people who I count on to tell me when I'm off the wall, when I'm fuzzy or long-winded or, simply, wrong. To be honest, it's also important that they offer occasional encouragement and praise. It is indeed a blessing to be able to rely on such terrifically good friends: Jay Mandle, Joan Mandle, Louis Ferleger, Joshua Markel, Eva Gold, Jo-Anna Moore, Michael Moore, Iz Reivich, and Burt Weltman. I would also like to thank Arnold "Skip" Isaacs for some helpful comments and considerable encouragement.

Academics need ballast to remain grounded. One group that helps me keep my head on straight is the blessedly non-faculty group I run with amongst the deer and turtle around Lake Fred: Bill Houck, Ken Johnson, Amanda Martin, Paul Chambers, Tim Lenahan, Joe Lo Sasso, Eric Page, Tim Kelly, and Julie Bowen. Another group includes those from the Vietnam Veterans of America Chapter 228 whom I have come to know and admire over the years, most particularly Patrick and Patti McGarvey and Ed Den Braven.

Temple University Press has been most supportive over the years. It's a great pleasure to work with them, particularly with Michael Ames, my editor and the press's editor-in-chief. Michael is a most simpatico professional; his editorial assistance has been inestimable.

Lastly, as always, there is family. Back in those Sixties, my cousin Mal Sumka told me that blood was thicker than water—we argued a lot back then. But it was always out of love on both sides. I've been fortunate to have had such bonds with members of my family. I'd like to make special mention of my aunt, Ceile Lyons, without doubt the smartest in my family, who taught me the art of storytelling. My wife, Mary Hardwick, has always been my partner; she has shown great patience in tolerating my obsessions, particular those times when my body was there but my head was off revising text. I feel particular pleasure in the ways in which my older stepchildren, Jennifer Zelnick and Nate Zelnick, as they have constructed their worlds, have entered mine, made it in part theirs, and offered me considerable assistance and at times inspiration to go forward. And Max, now thirteen, well, he reminds me that dads who publish books are still just dads.

Of course, none of the above are responsible for any of the views expressed in these essays.

Earlier versions of several chapters have appeared as:

"Yuppie: A Contemporary American Keyword." *Socialist Review,* January/March 1989.

"The Hidden Dangers of Yuppie Bashing." *The UTNE Reader,* July/August 1989.

"Peggy Noonan, Conservative Baby Boomer." *Socialist Review,* January/March 1992.

Class of 66: Living in Suburban Middle America. Temple University Press, 1994.

"Another Sixties: The New Right." *Viet Nam Generation,* 1994.

"New Left, New Right, New World." *Viet Nam Generation,* Summer 1995.

"Clinton, Vietnam and the Sixties." *Viet Nam Generation* 7.1–2 (1996).

New Left, New Right, and the Legacy of the Sixties

1

The Sixties

If you piled in front of you all of the dozens and dozens of books—popular histories, scholarly monographs, memoirs, biographies—and then watched all of the televised documentaries on the 1960s, you would get a remarkably consistent picture of that remarkable decade. The picture would focus on the Kennedys, the civil rights revolution, the Indochinese war, student activism, the New Left, the hippie counterculture—"sex, drugs, and rock 'n' roll"—the momentous events of 1968 (two assassinations, Tet, Chicago, Nixon's election), and a consideration of how and when, if ever, the Sixties ended.

I experience the consequences of this dominant picture each time I require the students in my course on the 1960s to interview a half dozen baby boomers. They return with the following lament: "I don't think I'm finding the right people." "What do you mean?" I ask, fully aware, from past experience, of why they're confused. "The people I talked to didn't do any of the things we're reading about; they weren't really part of the Sixties. I can't seem to find people who went to Woodstock, were real hippies, or who paid any attention to civil rights or the war. They just seemed to have ignored all that." "Ah," I calmly reply, "now you're learning about the difference between History with a capital *H* and actual life."

My point is not either to deny the centrality or to denigrate the impact of movements conventionally associated with the 1960s; in fact, I was a part of most of them and continue to value *most* of their legacy. It is, rather, to point to a distortion of historical reality, a simplification of how a particular generation—baby boomers—experienced a particular decade—the 1960s—and of how that dynamic interaction impacted on the American polity and culture then, since, and forthcoming.

The treatment of the Vietnam War offers one apparent qualifier to my Sixties critique. Considerations of the generational aspects of the war establish a great divide—those who served, those who protested. This is one of those rare instances when commentary focuses on social class. Those who served in Vietnam are portrayed as blue-collar grunts, the American proletariat and subproletariat, the white, black, and brown workingclass who lacked the influence to avoid the draft. Those who protested are characteristically presented as affluent college students whose idealistic motives for protesting seem subverted by their self-interest. The grunts sweat in the boonies; the protesters spit on returning vets in airports. This picture, initially constructed by James Fallows's "What Did You Do in the Class War, Daddy?" distorts the historical reality through a dualistic simplification.

This Vietnam dualism sits uncomfortably with the dominant myth of a Woodstock baby-boom generation. It suggests that the Vietnam vet experienced an in-country version of the generational war—drugs versus booze, longhairs versus crews, rock 'n' roll versus *Your Hit Parade*. Think of *Platoon* and *Good Morning, Vietnam*. When they returned home, *after* being spat upon, vets created their own version of the Sixties; one need only examine any documentary shot of Vietnam veterans in the 1970s and 1980s, true children of the Sixties. But since only a minority of them, a quite distinctive and significant minority, opposed the war, some generational discrepancies remain. It's as if we had a main story, from the Kennedy assassination through Woodstock, on the screen with a box of Vietnam both shaping the dominant discourse and offering a variation on a common theme.

My own argument is that we need to construct a generational portrait concerning both the Sixties and Vietnam that, at the least, begins with a triad: those who served, those who protested, those who did neither. If we want to move away from Sixties mythology we need to understand that there were at least two (I'll shortly add a third) highly visible and sometimes overlapped subgenerations—the GIs and the protesters—but also a probably larger group of mostly white, middle-class, suburban youth who cultivated their own gardens, dated, played sports, married, pursued careers, worried about insurance, thrilled to the Apollo moon landing, and were the generational component of what Richard Nixon proclaimed "the great silent majority." They tried, not always successfully, to avoid and ignore the major public and social issues of the day; regarding Vietnam, they often had the political pull to avoid serving there, especially through National Guard or reserve service.

So, at the very least, we need to reconfigure the generational dimensions of the Sixties to include what I call, in a recent book, "the silent-majority baby boomers." This group has not been unaffected by the dominant events of the decade, but it has experienced more continuity than discontinuity. Its members have been transformed as if behind their own backs, despite their own desires to sustain mainstream lives. They are certainly the people my students were finding when I sent them out to interview baby boomers.

To this now more variegated generation I must add an additional group. When all the shouting died down, when the last Mobilization headed back to the buses, when the hopes of Woodstock Nation were dashed against the forces of Altamont and the deaths of rock stars too numerous to list, when the utopian moment called the Sixties began to recede, there remained another ideological vision, another and alternative utopia whose moment would not come until the election of Ronald Reagan in 1980. A powerful conservative movement grew during the 1960s, a rising New Right that initially seemed to be the wave of the future, the proper fit for a new generation, gathering at the Sharon, Connecticut estate of William F. Buckley, Jr., filling the old Madison Square Garden to cheer on the candidacy of Barry Goldwater. As David Keene, later chair of the American Conservative Union, recalls from his student days during the Sixties, "We knew that these people who were out there rioting in the streets were handing us the country" (PBS's *Making Sense of the Sixties,* part 4). If we determine influence by who won, the New Right baby boomers, such as Newt Gingrich, can make at least as much of a claim to significance as their New Left rivals, especially as measured by the second eruption of the Reagan revolution in 1994.

It may be fruitful to consider the 1960s as a period in which two rival utopian challenges were posed to what British historian Geoffrey Hodgson calls the liberal consensus, a mix of welfare-state, American exceptionalism and anti-Communism. Such a consensus rested on the assumption, rooted in modernization theory, that economic matters had been resolved; that all that remained was merely technical finetuning; that, indeed, as Daniel Bell noted in his much criticized, seldom read, book, we had reached "the end of ideology." This technocratic vision, perhaps best personified by Camelot's Secretary of Defense Robert Strange McNamara, clashed with a variety of cultural dissenters from southern agrarians to Woody Guthrie, Erich Fromm, and Lewis Mumford.

But during the 1960s, resistance to what new leftists called corporate liberalism mobilized at both ends of the ideological spectrum. Both New Left and New Right championed the individual, savagely attacked the alienation and deadliness of industrial civilization, and evoked images of beloved communities that appeared to establish harmonies between antinomian and communitarian traditions. Both generational movements sought and found new heroes, figures who stood against the herd, albeit from virtually opposite positions. Consider Bob Moses of SNCC (the Student Nonviolent Coordinating Committee) and Barry Goldwater as examples, or C. Wright Mills and William F. Buckley, Jr. Although it sounds almost obscene to many ears, the fact remains, as E. J. Dionne, Jr., has so brilliantly argued, that the two youth movements shared a surprising number of passions and values.

So we can now reconstruct the Sixties generation as follows: a New Left/countercultural elite; a New Right elite; a more apolitical "silent majority" mass; Vietnam veterans, cutting across all three of these categories. And then some.

We need to consider three additional planes for a more complete picture. First, there is the issue of race and ethnicity. The distinctive role of African American baby boomers, whose most prominent members joined SNCC, the Congress of Racial Equality (CORE), youth branches of the NAACP, and later, the Black Panthers, must be right at the center of consideration. For one thing, to many white activists, inspiration came from such quarters, ranging from central concepts of the beloved community and participatory democracy to ways of being and acting, for instance, rhythm 'n' blues, denim, slang.

And the African American vanguard—the very use of the hyphenated identity—marks a shift toward multiculturalism, to a greater appreciation, at its best, of the incredible diversity within our culture. "Black is beautiful" opened the door to Spanish-speaking peoples, to Native Americans, to Asian Americans, indeed, to all non-Wasps.

Of at least equal weight is the matter of gender. The 1960s generation, more than any previous, has been shaped by the challenge of sexual equality, the coming to grips with what Betty Friedan called "the problem with no name." The Sixties would be the last period, assuming Margaret Atwood's fable remains science fiction, in which one could universalize male experience and marginalize "the other." Even New Right baby boomers such as Peggy Noonan have feminist behaviors and values intertwined, albeit uncomfortably, with their cultural conservatism.

Finally, there is the matter of age. It is one thing to consider the experience of the baby-boom generation in light of the events associated with the 1960s. But as a number of studies demonstrate, those events were by no means exclusively, or even in some significant instances predominantly, shaped by baby boomers. The peace movement and antiwar sentiment are cases in point. Older Americans were more opposed to the Vietnam War than were the young; and leadership in the peace movement included a remarkable number of less boisterous, less telegenic personalities born before 1946, often *considerably* earlier. One factor that distinguished New Right from New Left was its much more adult nature, the greater degree to which grown-ups initiated and dominated conservative youth and campus groups.

So, the outline for our story is now set. The 1960s generation must be understood as a diverse and contradictory bunch—isn't that always the case?—ideologically driven by two visions, numerically dominated by those on the sidelines, marked by the great divides of Vietnam, race, and gender. Plus we need to keep in mind that it would be historically inaccurate to ascribe the Sixties exclusively to a generation. So many of the key voices were World War II babies or children of the late Thirties—Todd Gitlin, Tom Hayden, Bob Moses, Mary King, Robin Morgan, Abbie Hoffman; so many others—Dave Dellinger, Bill Buckley, Mollie Yard, Benjamin Spock—were considerably older.

With all of this in mind, allow me to offer, in the form of questions, a set of themes that will drive this book.

The first question was initially voiced by John Dos Passos in *USA*—"All right we are two nations"—and more recently by Rodney King—"Can't we just get along?" The shift in context, from the Sacco-Vanzetti trial to the South Central LA riot, from prejudice against turn-of-the-century immigrants and trade unionism to a focus on race and racism, is at the core of this question. From the election of FDR to the late 1960s, the New Deal–driven politics of growth forged a coalition of working- and middle-class people, non-Wasp outsiders, joined by welfare-state benefits that created winners but no losers. The best examples of this would be Social Security retirement benefits and the GI Bill. There were fissures in the coalition; for example, it usually had to trim its sails to limit the power of the southern Democrat–Republican conservative coalition. Thus, labor felt frustration, and blacks got just the crumbs. But the coalition held, built on a multicultural ideal—the patrician Roosevelt mixing with Sidney Hillman and Manny Celler, with Irish Democratic pols, Polish, Italian, and Slavic constituencies.

But in the 1960s, all hell broke loose. The Democratic metaphor—the people against the interests; the salt of the earth, the Joads, Copeland's common man lined up against the plutocrats, those on the Main Line referring to FDR as "that man"; the Wall Street/Main Street alliance—broke down. The largest subverter was the failing economy; stagflation created a zero-sum reward system antithetical to the Politics of Growth. But race and class were the battering rams generating what was initially called a backlash among white ethnics against black demands and gains. We remain in this framework today, plagued by debates about multiculturalism, Afrocentrism, English First, affirmative action, quotas. The question pertains to three levels of being: individual, group, nation. Martin Luther King, Jr., raised the first in the context of the other two, anticipating a day when an individual would be judged by character rather than by race. Our individualistic culture has great difficulty resolving the contradiction between our desire not to be reduced to a racial or ethnic category—"Just pay attention to me! I'm just me!"— and the realities of stereotypical thinking and behavior. As Tom and Mary Edsall brilliantly note, our nation has been defined by this racial divide since the mid-1960s. More recently the battle has been joined by concerns about the extent to which we can remain a nation, a unified people, as opposed to a string of autonomous categories, a plurality of victims denying legitimacy to the mainstream historical experience.

Earlier versions of this dilemma of pluralism and culture certainly exist—Randolph Bourne and Horace Kallen addressed it eloquently earlier in the century—but the contemporary tensions seem to be more intractable given the chronic stagnation of the economy. How can we judge Americans as discrete, unique individuals, respect and honor their respective heritages and cultural roots, *and* hold together as a common, unified people? As we approach the end of the twentieth century, this seems one of the questions posed by the movements of the 1960s.

A related, if less glaring, set of questions emerging from the Sixties is: What is love of country? Who is a patriot? How should love of country be expressed? What kinds of behaviors are unacceptable? It has always interested me that a Martin Luther King, Jr., is rarely described as a patriot, whereas an Ollie North is universally granted that description. Why is that? During the 1960s there was a question of how one expresses love of country. And it was very unsettling to many Americans. Granted a certain amount of historical amnesia concerning previous antiwar dissent, granted Paul Fussell's persuasive argument that the model for absurdist war was set during World War I, there was a generational clash—World War II dads recalling "the good war" versus Vietnam grunts returning from free-fire zones, snipers, mines, and tunnel complexes. *Full Metal Jacket*'s Private Joker sees no contradiction in wearing peace signs on his helmet, while Tim O'Brien's Cacciato walks away from the Nam to go to Paris. The dress rehearsal for Vietnam syndrome—another way of defining the question—included the controversy over Francis Gary Powers's refusal to kill himself when his U-2 went down and the kinds of absurdist definitions suggested by *Dr. Strangelove, Catch-22,* and *M*A*S*H*. How does our response to national sacrifice define our national character, our individual characters? Would we, like Nathan Hale, be willing to die for our country? GIs like Ron Kovic, Bill Ehrhart, and Philip Caputo all began with an Audie Murphy/John Wayne model, a Kennedyesque "ask not" sense of commitment. But submerged images of war as insanity erupted and have prevailed; the comic-book excesses of the *Rambo* films highlight such metaphors of madness.

The radical activists of the 1960s had an opportunity to challenge and transform conventional definitions of patriotism—expressed through a love so strong that it required opposition to practices that violated the historical essence of our polity and culture. In this sense, Dr. King stands as our most impressive twentieth-century patriot, alongside those who opposed the war to restore U.S. commitments to democracy and self-determination. But, alas, the radicalizing peace movements, increasingly influenced by anti-imperialist models, and too easily falling into the trap of anti-Americanism, let the issue slip away. Protesters opposed or felt ambivalent about carrying the American flag in demonstrations; some felt no conflict over identifying with the Viet Cong's National Liberation Front (NLF) banner. On a personal note, I can recall having a ferocious and frustrating (because I persuaded no one) argument over the use of the American flag in a fourth of July antiwar rally. The repressive environment of McCarthyism, the powerful, exclusive force of the notion of an "American way of life," the very concept of something being "un-American"—all generated their polar opposites. If we weren't the source of all goodness in the world, if we weren't the champion of the free world, then we must be the essence of the world's evil, the Imperialist Amerikkka. Extremes call forth extremes.

But the question remains unresolved, a source of a nervous anxiety, a defensiveness, that we see in the responses to Dan Quayle and Bill Clinton and in the reluctance of Americans to support a war call that is likely to yield significant loss of American lives. Grenada? Libya? Panama? The Persian Gulf? Low-cost wars, all the gains of a community bonding together in crises, none of the anguish. But we haven't resolved how to deal with Mr. Quayle, a war hawk who used family influence to get into the National Guard, the most respectable, middle-class way to duck Vietnam, or President Clinton, a liberal dove on the war who seems unwilling to affirm today what he acted on yesterday—his moral revulsion concerning Vietnam.

And, of course, the continuing controversy over MIAs suggests the presentness of the questions Vietnam provoked. We haven't been able to lay to rest those who didn't return, because we haven't found the proper sermon; we remain schizophrenic, sometimes simulating John Wayne—think Ronald Reagan—at other times returning, again and again, to the Wall, that extraordinary monument to needless sacrifice, that black granite gash to unheroic, minimalist patriotism. What are we willing to die for? asks war hero and conservative James Webb. Most Americans, since Vietnam, avoid the question nervously. Sarajevo screams to us; we avert our eyes.

Perhaps part of an answer yet to be fully formulated lies in our reponse to another question: What are we willing to *live* for? That takes us to the third of our themes and questions, shaped by what may turn out to be the most far-reaching of 1960s challenges—the struggle to achieve gender equality, the quintessential question of how men and women are to live together, relate to one another, define each other, and how this is to affect our children.

The second-wave feminists coined the problematical slogan, "The personal is political." In many ways such a catchphrase epitomizes the third unanswered set of questions: How are we to live? What is right and what is wrong, and how are we to determine the answers to such questions? What is private and personal, and what is social and political?

John F. Kennedy's career suggests a beginning. He pushed the envelope on the issue of public/private about as far as it could go. He was our first celebrity president, admired as much for his life-style—that key and most pernicious word—as for his policies. He sold his candidacy and then his presidency through his family. One couldn't pick up a copy of *Time* or *Look* or *Life* without finding a photo article on the Kennedy compound at Hyannisport, Jacqueline, her wardrobe, her hairstyles, the children, the brothers and sisters, *their* children, the high jinks and parties, the various homes and estates, the pets, and so on. Meanwhile, President Kennedy relied on the press to cover up his extramarital liaisons. Here was the quintessential hypocrisy, the politician using his private life for public gain but counting on the old-boy network of journalists and pols to keep his "other" private life from destroying his public career. The sad experiences of Teddy Kennedy suggest what has changed over the past quarter century.

The feminist charge that such dichotomizing of public and private was essentially hypocritical and an instrument to maintain gender privilege is overwhelmingly true. At the same time, we have experienced a movement toward what could be called the *People Magazining* of America. Daniel Boorstin told us many years ago about the concept of the celebrity, Andy Warhol's fifteen-minute star, the person famous for being famous. How does such a corruption of our culture connect with feminist concerns?

For one thing, the personal is *related* to the political, but it is *not* the political. Our culture swung from denying the obvious—that how one lives one's life has some bearing on how one is to be judged in the public sphere, that "Do what I say, not what I do" has no more persuasive power when said by politicians to voters than it ever did when expressed by fathers to their sons—and proceeded to a simplistic and ultimately dangerous blurring and confusion about different spheres. The political, the public, sphere has at its core the reality of power. There are aspects of such power relations in our everyday lives, including within the family. But to *reduce* the realm of intimacy, of affection, of children to power relations is to deny the right to privacy—to totalize, to politicize all of existence. The work of Michel Foucault takes this madness to epistemological levels.

Granting the mischief spawned by a conflation of public and private spheres, there remains the profound transformation of a cultural revolution, with roots in Abigail Adams's insistence on the gender implications of the Declaration of Independence, made visible during abolitionist-inspired antebellum challenges, and rising and falling after the securing of women's suffrage. The second-wave feminism of the 1960s cannot take credit for the monumental transformations and, yes, dislocations we still are living through. But the Sixties-based movement framed the issues and drove the message home in ways that have affected all parties.

We might say that sexism began to crumble with the demise of the housewife, a gendered category rooted in the separation of work from home, with a life span of not much more than one hundred years. The erosion was furthered by the inherent egalitarianism of our polity and, in particular, by the educational results of that commitment to equality. As I tell my male-chauvinist students, if you wanted to keep women under control, you should never have allowed them to enter coeducational schools. In a world driven more by brains than brawn, it was only a matter of time before the irrationality of what Betty Friedan called "the feminine mystique" came under attack.

It's not as if the saga is complete. Tailgate scandals, harassment, abuse, rape, glass ceilings—all persist. But the resistances are rearguard, and all the more ferocious for that fact. In a culture with deep and historical commitments to equal opportunity and to the importance of schooling, there is no way to prevent women from converting their educational credentials into work and career.

The problem is that we haven't, as a culture, figured out how to accommodate such a profound transformation. We are nervous about what it all means in terms of our children. Who is responsible? Who will take care of them? Awkward terms like "latchkey children" suggest part of the problem. We aren't sure what it means to be a man and to be a woman. What is inherent, genetic, constitutional? What is cultural, political/ideological?

To transpose Rodney King from matters of race to those of gender, we can ask, How can and will we get along so that there can be stable, loving ways to raise our children? What do we owe to our loved ones—parents, spouses, children, relatives—and how can we accomodate such familial commitments to our powerful desires for individual expression? The Sixties movements sharpened the contradictions of these questions; old antinomian urges erupted in a culture of abundance, a decade that spoke of not trusting older people, of questioning all authority, of doing one's own thing, of loving the one you're with. The essence of a culture of abundance, which as early as the 1920s required less than half of its work force to be engaged in production (e.g., manufacturing, mining, agriculture), is the value of pleasure. How does pleasure "fit" within traditional moral values?

The dress rehearsal was the Scopes trial and the era of flappers and hip flasks associated with the writings and life-style— that key word of the culture of abundance—of F. Scott Fitzgerald. A Victorian, super ego–driven work ethic had to come to grips with the new realities of a mass consumption economy. The good citizen now had to develop what Stuart Ewen calls "the psychic desire to consume," marking the emergence of a "commodotized individual." Mass production, (e.g., the assembly line) mandated mass consumption and therefore a need to eliminate, or at least to temper, a culture defined by "A penny saved is a penny earned," a culture rooted in frugality. To free up individuals from that cultural contraint, Madison Avenue had to spearhead the acceptance of pleasure as normal, beneficial, functional to our economy. The old Puritanism (actually its sclerotic ghost), which furrowed its brow at the thought that someone, somewhere was happy, had to go. What cultural analysts call the culture wars have been set in motion by this economic and cultural reality, what Daniel Bell calls "the cultural contradictions of capitalism."

The 1960s took the dress rehearsal of the Twenties, which had been stalled by the Depression and war and then awkwardly embraced during the postwar 1950s, and let it rip. In fact, as Elaine Tylor May demonstrates, it was precisely the reactionary qualities of the Fifties—the ultimately unsuccessful drive to push back the liberatory implications of this golden age of U.S.

capitalism—that made the Sixties eruptions so ferocious. The Fifties pushed hypocrisy to new levels. People married younger, had more kids (running against all demographic trends, which link affluence and education with later marriages and fewer children), and functioned in an official culture headed by Joe McCarthy, Cardinal Spellman, and Billy Graham, by *Father Knows Best* and Doris Day movies. But these "Dark Ages" were hedonistic in subterranean ways, not just in the deviant subcultures of the beats and bikers, but in the mainstream flirtation with Marilyn Monroe and the other breast goddesses, with the emergence of Hugh Hefner's *Playboy* success. As Barbara Ehrenreich argues in *The Hearts of Men,* both the male-dominated *Playboy* and beat philosophies fused hedonism with sexual promiscuity for men, only differing in their assessment of mass consumption. The stage was set for a fuller, angrier assault on the inconsistencies, the winks of the TV comics, the pillow talk but no action.

And this eruption, often categorized as the counterculture and ascribed to the hippies, at least equally shaped by the feminist and gay challenges, placed pleasure in the forefront: If it feels good, it is good; do it! We have yet to recover from such challenges. Much of our political life has been dominated by the ways in which Sixties hedonism disrupted the finally unsuccessful compromises of the postwar years. The battles over abortion undoubtedly rest on fundamental issues of right and wrong, good and evil, rooted in our views of human pleasure and the rights of individuals to pursue happiness in a culture of abundance. How are we to live? What's a marriage? What's sacred? Who's minding the children?

Despite their enormous differences, both New Left and New Right movements sharpened the contradiction between individual and group. Finally, how does doing your own thing differ from a free-market, laissez-faire individualism? Both movements had romantic utopias to resolve the antinomian dilemma of how to construct a society based on this radically separate individual: The New Left posited a communist-anarchist vision of a classless, postscarcity, posthistorical social order, often fused if not confused with hippie, preindustrial, non-Western attractions to anything from Native Americans to E.T. The New Right constructed a more nostalgic community, a morning in America, based on the small town, the frontier, the idealized family. In both instances, reconciliation was set off from the present or from any meaningful strategy of social change. In a few instances, utopian separatism resulted, hippie or Christian communes rejecting the traditional command to live *in* the world but not *of* it.

The last question pinpointed by the 1960s emerged from the environmental movement: How can humanity, how can a species with a *human* nature, exploit but not destroy the rest of nature? Certainly the roots of such a question take us back at least to the concerns of Blake, to those of Thoreau over the destructiveness of the industrial revolution, to the conservation movement of the Progressive Era. But I would mark the revived challenge as beginning with the publication of Rachel Carson's *Silent Spring* and, inspired by the countercultural valuing of the natural over the artificial, the cooperative over the competitive, the creation of *The Whole Earth Catalog* and the beginnings of Earth Days. We are a fundamentally different culture, facing fundamentally different questions, since ecological consciousness emerged during the 1960s. As in all of the questions associated with the 1960s, even those people most hostile to challenges based on race, gender, and nature have had to incorporate aspects of the challenges into their arsenals, into their defenses. Onetime segregationists defend civil rights as they attack affirmative action, patriarchal men support equal pay for equal work as they oppose abortion on demand, free marketeers applaud corporate sensitivity to environmental needs as they criticize regulation. We are *all* now civil rights advocates, *all* now in favor of gender equality, *all* now claiming to be environmentalists. It's only the "extremists" whom we oppose. Indeed, the marginalizing of the extremes establishes new consensual centers. With all the talk of the movement of the culture to the right during the 1970s, the Reaganite 1980s, and the Gingrich-driven mid-Nineties, part of which is true, there has been all too much underestimation of the ways in which the challenges of the 1960s, most of them rooted in early probes and pokes, so stirred the pot, so dislocated the culture, that the very plates on which we stand have moved, the questions that we ask have changed in fundamental ways. In this sense, there certainly has been a reaction. How could it be otherwise given the enormity of the challenges? But a culture is defined, not by its answers, but by its questions, by the dialogue, the discourse, the arguments that drive it, that define it.

Perhaps it would be useful to sketch the scale and scope of the challenges suggested by portraying everyday life, before and after, as lived, not in the hothouse subcultures of the Beltway or Marin County or Harvard Square or the suite at Trump Plaza, but in Middle America, a term whose very existence and meaning rests on the impact of the 1960s. Ben Wattenberg and Richard Scammon posited a blue-collar housewife in Akron, Ohio, to make their points about the limits—and the risks— of the Sixties provocations; let me use my own neighborhood in a South Jersey suburb to make my case about the extent to which the movements of the 1960s transformed our lives.

Our South Jersey suburbanite—let's say born in 1938 and therefore twenty-two when JFK was elected and fifty-nine now—gets up in the morning and it's garbage day. In contrast to 1960, he needs to separate his garbage into at least three bins *and* have a separate container for his newspapers. He gets annoyed when his wife, fifty-seven, tells him to wash out the cans and plastic bottles before dumping them into the appropriate bin. He's dying for a smoke. But the new rules of the house, mostly enforced by his teen kids, are no smoking indoors. Sometimes he grabs a smoke in the basement, especially in cold or rainy weather. When it's warm, he just goes into the backyard. Before getting to work he lights up, because his office is now smoke-free and he can only grab a smoke during his breaks. He knows this is for the best; he was just reading about the cancer death of the Marlboro Man, long gone from TV, but nevertheless he asks, given the stress of everyday life, can't he have some rights to this little pleasure?

Worse, he no longer can eat certain foods. Too much cholesterol, too fatty, too salty—feh! In the old days, he never gave any thought to the nutritional quality of what he ate or to the hazards of smoking or to how discarded tin cans and plastics just piled up and up. Recycling is now common sense to him, but . . . it *is* a bother.

His wife works full-time; after they got married, she stayed home until the oldest kids were in school and then started working part-time in an office. But they could use the money—the two oldest are in college and the youngest kid is now a high-school junior. Our suburbanite helps out, making some dinners, even vacuuming occasionally. But the old division of labor still holds, uneasily. He's in the yard or, more typically, watching the ball game; his wife's making dinners, doing the laundry, washing dishes, cleaning house. She gets annoyed at him, especially when he's messing up the den with potato chips and diet sodas; he sometimes gets nostalgic for "the old days," for how it was with his old man— king of his castle, lord of his manor, at least so it seemed. He wonders.

He drops his daughter off at the high school (her car is in the shop) and notices that the once all-white campus has more than a smattering of black kids, and some Hispanics, and a mix of Asians—Filipinos, Koreans, Chinese, Indians, Vietnamese. He is dazzled by this, a little disturbed, especially when he recalls snippets of scenes when foreigners were speaking their own languages, "jabbering." Why can't they learn English? He doesn't notice that all of the students speak only English. And he worries about his daughter's future—it ain't like when he came out of school in '56. Jobs are scarce and college is getting expensive. He tends to blame the minorities and affirmative action, which he views as reverse discrimination.

Back in the 1950s and 1960s, he was openly prejudiced although critical of southern segregation and groups like the Klan. But he thought King and the civil rights folks were troublemakers; "we don't have any problems up here," he thought. Now he has reconstructed his past views and thinks that the civil rights revolution was good for the country—he believes in treating people equally, as individuals—and that people like King were right. But he thinks things have gone too far the other way and is particularly concerned with the rising crime situation, which he identifies with blacks. At the very same time, without any sense of contradiction, he admires and watches Bryant Gumbel and Bill Cosby, kids his wife about loving Oprah and Montel, and says he would support Colin Powell for president if he ran.

Some incidents in his kid's school and, even worse, guns and drugs in the nearby, more inner-city high school, upset him. His house has an expensive security system and he uses "the club" in his car. He takes such anticipation of crime as the way it is, but feels some anger when he recalls a less frightened, less crime-ridden culture. As he drives, he locks his doors nervously.

He worries about the culture. His daughter is a good kid, but she seems to either be watching MTV or going off to work or clubbing. He rarely sees her; she's been working twenty to thirty hours a week at the mall since her sophomore year. She needs him for big items, car insurance, but for the most part she covers her own costs. He both likes that and is made uncomfortable by it. They only eat together occasionally, since he, his wife, and their daughter have conflicting schedules.

When he thinks of how much the world has changed since he was a young man, he is less bewildered by all the technological changes (the computers, VCRs, cellular phones, camcorders) or even by the global political changes (the collapse of Communism) than by the ways in which his upbringing hasn't prepared him for the changes and adjustments within his everyday life.

He used to worry about his kids marrying within their faith; now he's more concerned with when and whether they'll marry at all. More than half his friends are divorced at least once; same with his kids' friends' parents. He has nieces and nephews in their middle thirties still not married, or married with no desire for kids. What's with them? Moreover, he worries about the sexual promiscuity—okay, he recalls his own adventures—but the kids seem so damn *casual* about it, like having a snack, for chrissakes! And there's AIDS—he never had to worry about that. Knock on wood, his marriage is okay, but if it failed, he dreads the very thought of dating, being at risk. And he shudders at the idea that one of his kids might turn out to be gay or lesbian. God forbid! One of his sons doesn't seem to date much, never cared for sports, but . . . he's afraid to ask, to even consider the possibility. He believes in being tolerant, feels he's grown up politically since his teen years when he would joke about rolling faggots in the movie theater bathroom. Live and let live, but homosexuality gives him the shivers. It's disgusting—despite his awareness, from talks with his daughter, that they're just people.

In some ways he lives in a more attractive world than that of his youth; for example, he loves the fact that he can rent movies, record stuff; he finds the new mall a great place for bargains. When he was a kid, he lived in what was still a small town sprouting development housing; now it's a suburb.

Back in his world of 1960, we were a society of one-third suburbs, one-third cities, and one-third small towns. Our political voices, urban voices, were still lunch-bucket machine pols like Daley in Chicago. Now the cities are colored—he rarely goes there—and the rural areas are shrinking. Half the voters he encounters are now suburban.

He goes to the movies that evening with his wife; the 5:45 show is half-price. He barely notices that the romantic lead— Al Pacino, or is it DeNiro?—is Italian, dark, swarthy or that in the preview, Barbra Streisand, who he feels intimidated by but finds sexy, has a big honker. Movie stars in his youth were all Waspy; if they weren't, they changed their names, fixed their noses, straightened their hair. None of that holds, since civil rights folks proclaimed "Black is beautiful," opening the door to a plurality of beauty. He doesn't recall any of this, taking for granted that those who once could only play gigolos or sidekicks now are romantic leads.

When he comes home he turns on the tube; on the cable stations, especially the comedy hours, he is amazed at the language—nothing is censored, everything is permissible. (Even on T-shirts.) And the infotainment shows and the talk shows—even the local news—seem sex obsessed. Always with the crazies—the guy who cheats on his wife with his sister, his niece, and his dog! "Aren't there any normal people out there?" he thinks to himself. He remembers Jack Paar getting kicked off the air for mentioning the w.c. and laughs to himself. "That was ridiculous, but aren't we taking this free speech stuff too far?"

Certainly those who aren't European white males might experience such cultural changes differently—his wife, his kids, his Cuban or Korean or Jamaican neighbors. But the point of this little profile is to suggest the tip of the iceberg of changes in attitude and behavior, in feelings and values, demanded of Americans as they were crystallized during the 1960s. We have been asked, sometimes required, to change in fundamental ways. The issue is not whether such changes have been necessary and beneficial, both to the society and to the individual. My emphasis is on the magnitude of the changes as they touch the everyday life of individuals—from issues of recycling and of carcinogenic chemicals in our food to the demands of living in a multicultural society to the very intimate issues of sexual identity, marriage, family, love, children.

The 1960s marked a watershed in the emergence of a culture of abundance; at the same time, it brought forth a set of economic crises—the stagflation of the Seventies, the uneven economic surge of the Eighties, especially the erosion of the middle classes—that exacerbate the inevitable tensions provoked by that culture. The Sixties was both another moment in the assertion of antinomian impulses and communitarian,

perfectionist visions *and* a coming together of cultural assaults on what appeared to be dysfunctional and thus increasingly hypocritical restraints on human desire. It was
also part of the ongoing American battle over fulfilling the
promise of the Declaration of Independence. All (white) men
created equal, indeed! The Sixties inspired oppressed groups
to demand their due and to demand it "now"—all following
Martin Luther King, Jr.'s assertion of "why we can't wait."

At the same time, we can see some of the problems associated with the 1960s and its legacy—what conservatives call
"special interests," and what astute observers like Tom and
Mary Edsall see as undermining the New Deal Democratic
Party coalition: the assertion of rights, the focus on victimization, the denial of responsibility through charges of "blaming the victim," the fears of fragmentation, of a loss of unity
and a common American identity.

Part of the conservative success associated with Ronald
Reagan and his mid-Nineties devotees rests on a resentment
over the challenges to a mythic unity that truly denies participation on the basis, especially, of race and gender. But the
New Right has made its own accommodations to inclusion.
Lee Atwater's call for a big tent cannot be reduced to opportunism; there has been a shift of the center leftward. The
claims of a rightward drift since the Sixties underestimate the
degree to which the entire cultural conversation has shifted
radically. The challenges were so fundamental, so traumatic,
that we have been weathering simultaneously acceptance and
regression—the "I'm not a feminist, but . . ." syndrome. As
such, the limits of conservative success in establishing a new,
long-term coalition, making permanent the Reagan revolution, rest on the limited attraction to reaction—to racism à la
David Duke or Pat Buchanan, to Christian Coalition fanati-

cism, to a denial of fairness to all parties, including gays. I say this with full awareness of the 1994 election. I continue to believe, as the response to the 1992 GOP convention in Houston demonstrated, that the American Middle fears and rejects reaction.

In what has to be short of a final analysis—we are still too close, things are still too much in motion, the past of the Sixties remains the present—the 1960s and its movements and agendas rest on a kind of two-ring circus performing before an audience. The two rings are the ideological cultural elites—one left wing, one right wing—presenting critiques of the welfare-warfare state from the vantage point of antibureaucratic, romantic utopian visions.

The left-wing version, more in the Sixties spotlight, assaulted the marketplace; the right-wing story, at first in the shadows, hit statism. Both imagined a revitalization of the individual and of liberty; both longed for a community. Both offered heroic alternatives to the humdrum rat race, the gray-flanneled, buttoned-down, organization-man conformity. Che Guevara and John Galt, Woodstock Nation and Robinson Crusoe, book-end critiques of the merely bourgeois pleasures, of the seemingly contradictory commitment of most Middle Americans to conservative values and liberal programs, to the babel of a mixed economy. The cultural elites were at their best in attacking the hypocrisies, the cultural contradictions, of 1950s-style capitalism.

In fact, when we examine the late 1950s and early 1960s, we discover that the embryonic New Right and New Left broke bread together at the White Horse Tavern in the Village and at other places where all those dissatisfied with the dullness of the Eisenhower years gathered. Jack Kerouac's hostility to the New Left movements, the flirtation of right-wing libertarians like Murray Rothbard with the antiwar, New Left movement, the shift of Karl Hess from New Right to New Left, the flip-flops of David Stockman, and later of David Horowitz and Peter Collier—all suggest the parallels between the two cultural challenges. And to examine the legacy of the 1960s is to note the ways in which New Left and New Right challenges changed the cultural discourse. We will never be the same on issues of race and gender, on all categories of difference—in this regard, and possibly no other, the postmodernists are correct—and on issues of the natural world. And structures of hierarchy, of authority and respect deeply eroded. So when Dan and Marilyn Quayle lambast the Sixties for "indulgence and self-gratification," insisting that "not everyone demonstrated, dropped out, took drugs, joined in the sexual revolution or dodged the draft," they speak only a partial truth. First of all, they focus too much of the blame for permissiveness on the counterculture and not enough on the business culture so sacred to New Right ideologues. Madison Avenue has done more to subvert traditional values and behaviors than any vanful of hippies and radicals could hope to accomplish. A culture of abundance, an economy within which less than half of the work force is engaged in production of commodities, an economy that *requires* mass consumption and, therefore, a liberation from old-fashioned attitudes about money, work, and pleasure drives the cultural contradiction of capitalism; hippies and SDSers only served as an unintentional vanguard. What the Quayles, Newt Gingrich, and other conservatives refuse to affirm is that the New Left movements deserve credit for spearheading the opening up of the American dream to blacks, women, seniors, the disabled, and for raising all the appropriate and pressing questions about our environment. We have been changed for the better by such movements; that the process has not been completed should scarcely surprise us. We've only had a generation to come to grips with the realities of race, gender, life-style, and the natural environment. Our middle-aged guy from the New Jersey suburbs has changed, sometimes despite himself, often behind his back, on such matters. And he grumbles about it—a lot.

New Rightists in the 1960s were inspired by Hayek's anti-statist *The Road to Serfdom* and by Milton Friedman's free-market writings. As much as the New Left worshipped anti-market, postscarcity planning in which, à la Marx, products would be distributed from each according to ability, to each according to need, New Right conservatives assumed that the market would resolve all problems through Adam Smith's invisible hand.

As the economy turned downward and flattened out, free-market arguments gained in influence; however, the concept that private vice will yield public virtue remains the Achilles' heel of conservative ethics. The market remains in the saddle, for the most part in response to the crisis of the welfare state (i.e., the breakdown of the Politics of Growth), but its abstract attractiveness is already beginning to wither in the application, for example, in the former Soviet bloc economies. The New Left's "new socialist man," the no longer prehistorical selfless producer, collapsed before the realities of actual, in-this-world human behavior; sometimes even Fidel Castro seems to have seen the light. The same is true for the conservative's naive faith in the entrepreneurial spirit, although George Will may not get that message before the next century arrives.

Where New Right success rests on Sixties experience is in the area of law and order. My Northfield man and his family live only a weak version of what city folks—black, white, and all others—experience. The ongoing sense of insecurity, of fear—of senseless violence, of rape and assault, of drug-driven crime, of school kids with knives and guns, of teachers stabbed and shot—of a near hysterical uncertainty about what any and every society *must* provide to all of its citizens: peace, public order, a safe environment.

The New Right, beginning with George Wallace's racist populism, sharpened with Nixon and Agnew's "law and order" demagogy, and triumphant with Reagan's "tough on crime" policies, has responded to a growing public concern about violent crime. The New Left's legacy has been satisfied with a "blaming the victim" argument. At its worst, leftists and liberals have romanticized criminals as antibourgeois heroes, the Pretty Boy Floyds of Woody Guthrie's folk tales, Bonnie and Clyde as Robin Hoods, stealing from the banks and helping the poor. Guthrie warbled, "You'll never see a outlaw drive a family from its home." He didn't live to see crack posses terrorizing tenement families. Conservatives too often play the race card shamelessly, but Sixties activists often made it easier by glamorizing the Black Panthers, calling police "pigs," and flirting with Hell's Angels, even Charles Manson.

So a central legacy of the 1960s, one that both radical and conservative ideologies have failed to remedy, is the sense of personal insecurity. We pay an enormous price in our central nervous system. We only notice when we are fortunate enough to visit a safe environment, only too often beyond America's borders. We see what a price we pay for our level of crime. We now know that the conservative solution—full jails, long sentences, capital punishment—does not work; are we safer now than in 1980 when we had one-third the number of prisoners? But the radical focus on structural explanations—poverty, racism, unemployment—remains a necessary but not sufficient response.

Finally, about our foreign policy. At the outset of the 1960s, John Fitzgerald Kennedy evoked an ambitious, idealistic, martial stance, a generational call to "ask not." The nation and its youth responded, in Indochina. The New Left elite attacked knee-jerk anti-Communism and introduced a healthy dose of self-criticism in our own motives and foreign policy behavior, for example, the tragedies of U.S. diplomacy that historian William Appleman Williams analyzed. Later in the decade, too many activists, enraged by the ongoingness of the Vietnam War, became mirror images of superpatriots, with the United States becoming the carrier of evil to the world. New Rightists maintained the absolutist Cold War faith, Reagan's evil empire, Whitaker Chambers's moral crusade. Neither group anticipated what has occurred. While leftists romanticized Ho Chi Minh—who, along with the NLF was "gonna win"—conservatives demonized, evoked dominoes, saw gulags at every turn, and rallied to the most despicable Third World dictators in South Africa, Iran, Chile, and dozens more.

But behind everyone's back, instead of dominoes falling (which, in anticipation, the Left cheered and the Right feared), the U.S. loss in Vietnam masked the more significant transformation of East Asia, the emergence of the ASEAN nations—the little tigers of Malaysia, Singapore, Hong Kong, Taiwan, and South Korea, Indonesia, Thailand, India—all experiencing impressive economic growth. And all repudiating both left and right utopias, instead fashioning their own versions of a state-sponsored, rarely democratic capitalism. Neither Paul Sweezy nor Milton Freidman have proved very helpful in this regard.

So what is the legacy of the 1960s? What has been the historical role and place of the baby-boom generation? Certainly the roots of all of the questions and themes associated with the Sixties go back to the very beginnings of the culture of abundance, the turn of the century into the dress rehearsal of the 1920s. Many of the dilemmas rest on deeper historical tensions based on our distinctive religious heritage, our particular ways of being heirs of the Protestant Reformation, our struggles with the consequences of radical individualism: How can a stable society be constructed from the conscience-centered, antinomian individual? How can a priesthood of all believers hold together?

When one adds to the brew the lubricants of desire and pleasure, of a modern capacity to fulfill dreams, and then when one factors in the newly legitimated demands of stigmatized, oppressed groups for access to those dreams, and then, to add a twist, forces all parties to consider the limits to the environment's capacity to offer unending fruits, an infinite array of commodities—*all* of this only begins to suggest the legacy of the 1960s.

The last word must go to our Jeffersonian voice, to our Lincolnian sense of responsibility; we face the challenge to grow up, to cast off the immaturities of gender privilege and ethnocentrism, the childishness of always blaming the other, acting as if we are each an island unto ourselves, as if our suburban cocoons can protect us from our nightmares, as if we aren't already interdependent—interdependent electronically, and therefore economically; interdependent in terms of Chernobyls and TMIs and ozone layers.

The best of the 1960s offered a variety of voices to help us address such dilemmas. To respond to that challenge will require that we incorporate the best of contradictory traditions as we recognize the need to move past their respective dogmas. To move past the Sixties, we still must come to grips with its challenges, its passions, its commitments, its blindness.

2

How Did We Get to the Sixties?

The 1920s served as a kind of dress rehearsal for the Sixties, although a case can be made for the pre–World War I years when bohemian, nationalist, and radical currents brought forth such rebels as Eugene Debs, Big Bill Haywood, Margaret Sanger, John Reed, Mabel Dodge Luhan. As Martin J. Sklar has argued, the Twenties marked the emergence of a service economy, within which more than half the working population, for the first time in human history, was not engaged in the primary production associated with agriculture, mining, or manufacturing. The promise of capitalism anticipated by Adam Smith in his visit to a pin factory and by Karl Marx in the *Manifesto,* the ways in which the application of power to production could vastly increase the size of the economic pie—could, indeed, challenge the permanence of scarcity. This promise of abundance came closer to fulfillment in the America defined by Henry Ford's assembly line, his much-celebrated high wages, and the development of a mass-consumption industry (Madison Avenue) to insure that the flood of consumer goods—radios, appliances, cars—would move off the shelves. Alas, the imbalances of the 1920s economy, the weakness of organized labor in particular, led to the market crash, Black Friday, and consequently to the Great Depression. But the coordinated national economy, studied by Herbert Hoover's Committee on Social Trends, now existed, albeit without the Keynesian manipulations to sustain the demand side.

The cultural contradictions of capitalism, the tensions so well defined by Daniel Bell as the subversion of production's work ethic by mass consumption's necessary hedonism, become salient during the 1920s. The Jazz Age offered us a relatively small elite of educated youth experimenting with what later would be called life-style concerns, such as sexual permissiveness, flapper insouciance, hip-flask defiance of prohibition, the white use of a sterotyped black hedonism as role model for a looser, less inhibited, more joyous life. Scott and Zelda; the Babe; the notion of the celebrity, the person famous for being famous, the valuing of styles of consumption over productive accomplishment—all deepened the contradictions that, closer to our own era, would be characterized as "work hard, play hard."

The Great Depression sidetracked this set of developments to a considerable but not total extent. But the war goosed the economy, which brought forth in the period from 1946 to 1973 the unprecedented golden age of capitalism during which the American utopia of what I prefer to call middle classlessness—the rich, mostly middle-income people, and no poor; the American alternative to Marxism—seemed to approach fruition. The response to the Depression established the political formula that harnessed the entrepreneurial anarchy of the market to the empathetic supervision and guidance of the emerging American welfare state. The New Deal established new contracts and parameters for the American dream. It offered stopgap assistance to help people keep their homes and farms, public works projects and other government-as-the-employer-of-last-resort jobs, regulation of the excesses of capitalist private interest, some economic planning, a social security system setting a floor below which no citizen would be allowed to fall, and guarantees of a more level playing field such that unions had a real shot at organizing workers. Of course, this breakthrough toward a welfare state, that is, a society with income inequalities but no poverty, was achieved more in promise than delivery. But it was enough to give the Democrats thirty-six years of overwhelmingly majority rule as the presumed party of the people, the common man, the working stiff, the immigrants, the blacks.

Everyone knows that it was World War II, not the New Deal, that ended the Depression. But the New Deal established a framework, the beginnings of what Godfrey Hodgson calls the liberal consensus, which the war economy and then the Politics of Growth of the Truman, Eisenhower, Kennedy, and Johnson administrations fleshed out. Hodgson's liberal consensus of the postwar years focuses on the uniquely liberating and democratizing qualities of U.S. capitalism. U.S. capitalism, through its productive capacity, makes radical challenges moot, with harmony, or at least countervailing interests, built upon a widening, thickening Middle America. In Hodgson's model—we see this epitomized by President Kennedy—problems are reduced to the technical; Keynes supercedes Marx. In this middle-classless utopia, all threats, logically, are external and alien. The Cold War stands as the arena within which U.S. capitalism has the obligation to demonstrate its superiority to archaic but dangerous ideologies—communism in particular—through military defense and economic expansion.

I do not believe that the dominant consideration driving economic growth in the postwar years was the Cold War. The military-industrial complex, symbolically born with the completion of the Pentagon during the war and shaped by the national security apparatus of CIA, Department of Defense, and National Security Council, certainly served as a kind of substitute industrial policy instrument, and it played a significant role in stimulating the economy. However, I would argue that the essential stimulus came from the civilian side, from what I jokingly call the SHMA complex: Suburbs/Highways/Malls/Autos. This civilian component of the Politics of Growth rests on the synergy of postwar suburbanization and its infrastructural requirements of highways, malls, and automobiles. One must add the democratization of education, especially as stimulated by that most significant of welfare state pieces of legislation, the GI Bill of 1944.

The GI Bill, as argued by Diane Ravitch, played a critical role in the expansion of the American middle class. It is especially significant in its successful challenge to the elitist fears that opening the doors of the academy to the children of immigrants, workers, and farmers would lead to the deterioration of higher education.

During the golden age of capitalism, the middle class became nearly two-thirds of the population. Home ownership, the best measure of American definitions of middle-class life, jumped from 44 percent in the mid-Thirties to 63 percent by the early seventies. As late as 1950 only 59 percent of Americans owned cars; the Interstate Highway Act of 1956, a Politics-of-

Growth success of a Republican administration and a Democratic Congress, served as catalyst toward the seven cars per ten inhabitants we became by the 1980s. An obvious measure of change with shorter term turnover is television. In 1947, there were seven thousand TVs in the land; within only three years seven million Americans had the capacity to tune in to Uncle Miltie on Tuesday nights. The very landscape of America changed, as eighteen million Americans moved to the suburbs between 1950 and 1960. It became our characteristic setting.

The industrial worker, formerly terrorized by the coal-and-iron police in Pennsylvania company towns, living from pay check to pay check, always fearing layoffs, now had union wages and benefits, attractive overtime possibilities. Using the GI Bill, he could fulfill the dream of home ownership, as Arthur Levitt and other development entrepreneurs built less costly suburban homes with low down payments and minimal interest rates. By the time John Fitzgerald Kennedy was elected president, it seemed as though, to many Americans, we had become "the affluent society," truly a people of plenty. Those left out, those Michael Harrington would describe as the "other Americans," seemed quite invisible, or at least a mere residue, soon to join their more fortunate fellow citizens in the crabgrass frontier of the suburbs.

So the first framework in understanding the Sixties is the remarkable if uneven prosperity spawned by the Democratic Party strategy of all winners with no losers—the Politics of Growth. Lyndon Johnson, as the Senate Majority Leader during the Eisenhower years, stands as the personification of this strategy, perceiving himself as Franklin Roosevelt's son and heir, committed, simultaneously, to enrich the rich and to end poverty, to build a Great Society, to invite everyone to a

Great Barbecue of Texas oil and gas magnates, defense contractors, SHMA industries and their collaborative unions, public employees, minorities, the old, the young, the sick.

It is useful to consider what America looked like before the golden age of capitalism. No Pentagon, no shopping malls, no TV, many fewer cars, no clover-leaf entry and exit routes to thousands and thousands of miles of highways. During the Fifties and Sixties, working people, unionized, protected to some extent with retirement pensions, could actually take vacations, maybe two weeks in a bungalow at the Jersey shore, maybe even buy a small boat. From the vantage point of the turn of the century, of the 1930s, this was an extraordinary turn of events. This is what made the Democrats so dominant—they could deliver the goods and they could do good.

Marty Jezer calls this period the "Dark ages," and in some very important ways it was. At the same time, one must emphasize how much this period offered to a majority of Americans. Yes, the suburbs could be stifling; they did look like little boxes made of ticky-tacky. But those living in them individualized, customized after moving in. Just drive through Levittown, Pennsylvania, and you'll see the shrubs and trees, the added rooms and decks, the personal touches of a generation of mostly first-time home owners.

It is also true that this process involved something of a conspiracy of banks and automobile manufacturers that destroyed public transportation and red-lined ethnic city neighborhoods, inducing the flight to the suburbs. And it depended on the artificially low energy costs of a time when the United States was number one and there was no number two, when regular gas cost less than thirty cents a gallon. And, most unfortunately, this movement toward the suburbs increased the isolation of African Americans moving to the cities, looking for opportunity, and finding themselves in deteriorating neighborhoods in cities facing declining tax bases. The pull toward the suburbs, the desire for space, for privacy, was also a push generated by racial bigotry, block-busting, and red-lining.

The Fifties were darker for those left out, and they seemed particular dim for many intellectuals oppressed by the conformity and mindless materialism they associated with the man in the gray-flannel suit, the organization man, the lonely crowd, the other-directed person, those enticed by hidden persuaders and intimidated by Joe McCarthy and his ilk.

One way to approach the Fifties is to juxtapose the post-war era with the New Deal years. Social change is driven by a certain optimism, a hopefulness, a feeling that one can fight city hall, that one can join with others to make history. More conservative, inward-turning periods do not share these expectations and instead focus on simply making a life, turning away from public matters that extend beyond one's immediate environment. As Herbert Gans reminds us, it's not as if most Americans become selfish or narcissistic in these insular times but that they have lower expectations of the capacity of citizens to affect the larger body politic. At such times, they tend to devote most of their time and energy to personal and family matters.

During the 1930s, a society virtually obsessed with something they started calling the American way of life found nourishment in the concept of "the people," a term the critic Kenneth Burke posited as having greater resonance than the more Marxist notion of "the proletariat" or "the working class" with most Americans. He was right. The era of the New Deal framed the more successful left-wing variant of a Popular Front, a symbol that spawned, among other things, a rediscovery of our popular musical roots—folk music. The folk music of the Almanac Singers, of Woody Guthrie and Leadbelly, the WPA reconstructions of local and state histories were a part of a retelling of the American story. This story, researched by scholars like Charles and Mary Beard and Vernon Louis Parrington, pitted the American people against those with little faith in democratic possibilities, from New England Puritans to robber barons. The plays of Clifford Odets and the novels of John Steinbeck reflect and enriched this populist story. The Joads, Okies, and Arkies, Dust Bowl survivors, *were* the people and they *would* endure.

It was this investment in the decision-making capacity of everyday people—what Henry Wallace, during the war, envisioned as the beginning of the "Century of the Common Man"—that inspired the political reform movements of the Thirties. As late as 1946, one can feel the lift of such a populist saga in the Academy Award-winning *Best Years of Our Lives,* as returning servicemen struggled to sustain the idealism of the New Deal era.

But the New Deal/Popular Front commitment to making history, rooted in its belief in the democratic capacity of everyday Americans, eroded after the war. The GI Bill was in many ways its finest moment. By 1948 Harry Truman's Fair Deal was a no deal, and extensions of the welfare state, such as health care, would have to wait at least several generations. What happened?

I would begin with imagery, from the Joads and Odets's Lefty to that sensuous hunk out of Tennessee Williams's imagination, Stanley Kowalski. Think for a moment of the imagery of the working stiff, the common man we associate with the Thirties; recall images of sit-down strikes, the kinds of roles the young Henry Fonda and Jimmy Stewart played.

Now there stands this brute, whom I prefer to characterize as the first Polish joke, the first powerful image of the working stiff as barbarous, crude, and positively fearsome. Polacks, in this case, are merely stand-ins for all working people. The imagery runs from Brando's Stanley to the more innocuous Chester A. Riley or the bombastic Ralph Kramden and then to Archie Bunker and hard-hat, Joe Six-Pak icons. Instead of heroic and enduring, the common man becomes a threat to civilization and culture. Can Stanley or Archie be the basis for a genuine democratic order? Would civil liberties, constitutional protections survive?

The blue-collar wives, from Alice Kramden and Peg Riley to Edith Bunker, love their not-so-sharp hubbies, mother them, often manipulate them in ways that allow them their "male pride." Their expectations, like those of the Fifties culture at large, remain low. What can one expect from such lummoxes, however beloved?

The mainstream liberal intellectuals of the postwar years tended to translate the second Red Scare, associated with Senator Joseph McCarthy, as a "revolt of the masses." The attacks on the newly established power of organized labor, big labor, meshed neatly with this new elitist cultural offensive. Brando's Terry Malloy in *On the Waterfront* turned out to be a nicer, more heroic prol than Stanley, but the focus of attention was on the corruption of the unions, the seeming pervasiveness of the Johnny Friendlys.

The Marxist tradition speaks of the need for an agency of social change. By the mid-Fifties, none was available, neither the workers nor the people. There was, instead, a celebration of a way of life, climaxed perhaps by Richard Nixon's famous kitchen debate with Nikita Khrushchev. The U.S. standard of living, during this golden age of U.S. capitalism, stood on a mountain of washers and dryers, dishwashers, toasters, TVs, cars, home improvement power tools, power boats, and garden and lawn paraphernalia.

The American people were the beneficiaries of this largesse; in some ways they were its very creators. But the crucial shift was from production to consumption, from life to life-style. It is in this sense that Ozzie Nelson matters; as viewers often remarked, "The man never works!" In fact, it didn't matter what kind of work he did; *Father Knows Best*'s Jim Anderson worked in insurance, but what did it matter? No one ever learned the details of the work he actually did; he merely had the kind of employment, as one could presume of old Ozzie, that allowed for a middle-class standard of living, that is, home ownership, suburban setting, housewife, and children.

This middle-class life-style, available to a significant proportion of the unionized working class, was the great carrot to the ideological conformity that characterized the 1950s. Elaine Tyler May is right to emphasize the reactionary qualities of Fifties family life—the earlier marriage ages, the larger family sizes, the cultural offensives to validate exclusively the white, heterosexual, male-headed, single-breadwinner suburban family. It was a reactionary time, fighting off changes that had their roots in the larger transformations of the earlier decades of the century. For example, if we were moving toward a fully coeducational system of public schooling and then higher education, how could we expect women to continue to return from high school or college to being "the little woman" standing behind her corporate or professional man? Betty Friedan would soon articulate the nature of this problem with no name, this glaring contradiction between preparation and production.

Yet one understands the pull of Fifties conformity. After all, the system was providing so many folks with more than they had ever dreamed possible. And it looked like there would be even more for their children. Hadn't Samuel Gompers, the old American Federation of Labor (AFL) leader, responded to the question of what the U.S. worker really wanted with "More"? And there was now more and then some.

I believe that the postwar years from 1945 through 1960, what we actually mean by the Fifties, was an era haunted by the concerns of Max Weber, the German social theorist so influential in precisely this period within the American academy. One of Weber's key notions was rationalization, the process by which society was increasingly subjected to the logic of bureaucracy, instrumentalism, rational procedure. Weber worried about this desacralization of life itself, what he called the disenchantment of the world. He anticipated the emergence of charismatic, demagogic leaders to offer solace from this rationalized environment.

Indeed there is a mixed message in the ways in which critics and observers characterized the 1950s. It was simultaneously an age of celebration and an age of anxiety, a period of enthusiasm about the seemingly permanent accomplishments of the Politics of Growth, of Keynesian economics, and an assumption of a certain inevitability to the rise of the welfare state. Modernization theory certainly dominated the social sciences of this period. And yet always, even if hidden in the shadows of McCarthyist conformity, there was anxiety, uncertainty, worry. "How I learned to stop worrying and love the bomb," joked the young Stanley Kubrick. One worry, of course, was the Cold War, the fear of Communist aggressions, the concerns about nuclear war, radiation fallout, strontium 90. This was not paranoia—there was a threat of global, nuclear war; the Soviets could behave recklessly, as they did in giving the North Koreans the green light to invade the South, or, under Khrushchev, in providing Fidel Castro with short-range nuclear missiles.

Although it is now fashionable to assume, on the basis of the collapse of Soviet Communism, that the U.S. policies during the Cold War were appropriate, correct, and, most importantly, successful, I suggest several caveats. First of all, we must distinguish two kinds of Cold War, the first an East-West struggle over Soviet control of Eastern and Central Europe, the second a North-South struggle over the decolonization of what came to be called the Third World. In Cold War I, the Soviets imposed their will, and we acquiesced, unwilling to risk war over their Iron Curtain rule. We sniped; we spied; we provoked occasionally; our ideological conservatives called for rollback and liberation; but, with the marginal exception of crises over Berlin, this East-West Cold War was over by 1948. The conservative historian John Lukacs used to argue that the most appropriate U.S. response to Soviet domination in Eastern Europe was a firm patience, understanding that historical forces, most particularly the force of nationalism, were on our side. And after forty-plus years of domination, it is striking how little acculturation the Soviets wrought, other than a kind of aversive conditioning.

Most striking to me are the ways in which the United States was taken in by the Soviets' bluff. Theirs was a remarkably weak, almost primitive economy, despite its impressive rates of growth during the 1950s. Michael Beschloss demonstrates in his stunning accounts of the Khrushchev era how the Soviets covered their gross inferiorities in all economic and technological, and therefore military, arenas. Khrushchev proclaimed, "We will bury you!" and we half believed him, an indicator of this decade of anxiety, of uncertainty, of self-doubt. We were the world's number-one power, the only nation with the capacity to attack, with maximum force, anywhere on earth, ushering in what Henry Luce appropriately called the "American Century," an era of remarkable economic success. Yet we were afraid that Khrushchev might be right, that the Soviet planned economy might outperform ours. In retrospect, this may be the most remarkable misperception of the entire postwar era.

As the William Appleman Williams school of U.S. diplomatic history has always stressed, U.S. policymakers believed that without expansion our system would be at risk, that, as Marxists stated, capitalism required imperialism. Of course, their formulation of this process was benevolent, one in which U.S. investments and trade enriched all parties. But there remains a telling lack of confidence in the power of economics among U.S. decision makers; and this lack of confidence, I suggest, marks an even more telling lack of maturity.

We see this particularly in what I call Cold War II, the tendency of U.S. policymakers to reduce Third World struggles for self-determination in a postcolonial world to East-West conflicts, finally, to Soviet machinations. The Truman Doctrine most fully embodies this tendency. Truman in effect declared that indigenous rebellions that could be characterized as Communist or Communist-inspired would be defined as equivalent to a Soviet invasion of an independent nation. As cautious, sober observers, such as Walter Lippmann, noted at the time, this was writing a blank check for interventionism, especially to preserve the status quo, to align the United States with any right-wing dictator who simply cried Communist subversion. Why did we fall for this trap, which would align us with the Somozas, Batista, the Shah, Syngman Rhee, Marcos, Mobuto, South African apartheid, and so many other despicable regimes? Jeane Kirkpatrick's neat little model of authoritarian vs. totalitarian isn't persuasive, since we had stronger ammunition than her argument suggests. The United States had the capital, the technologies, the organizational experience, the managerial smarts to seduce most impoverished nations toward our interests. We were competing with an ideal, varieties of statism (from Nasserism to African socialism to Soviet- or Chinese-style Communism) that still needed what we could supply—money, goods, expertise. What were we afraid of? We were afraid that we weren't, in fact, the more productive, the "better" way, the wave of the future. We feared Khrushchev's economic boasting because we weren't able to persuade ourselves—deep within—that the direction of modernization was not toward communist-style command economies. It boggles the mind in the light of 1989.

There were sober voices—Lippmann, Hans Morganthau, George Kennan, J. William Fulbright, George Ball—who understood; who knew how a mature world power should behave; who recognized that, given the cards we held, we had little need to react precipitously to every real or imagined Soviet challenge. The ideological Right wanted us to call the Soviets' bluffs militarily. They lacked confidence in the ability of the United States to demonstrate its superiority over time; as many astute observers have noted, they became mirror images of their enemies and believed the worst rhetoric about Soviet intentions, Soviet ambitions, Soviet achievements. And they did their best to bring parts of the Soviet system to our shores, fighting Communism with a brand of anti-Communism complete with its own star chambers, witch hunts, and repressive atmosphere.

This insecurity, this anxiously looking over the shoulder,

tells us much about the underside of the Fifties, those un-
dercurrents of dissent, criticism, and rebellion that would become the essence of the 1960s movements. Virtually all accounts of the roots of the 1960s discuss these prologues,
these hints and glimmers of movement. The academic and
popular literature of the Fifties, the works of Vance Packard,
William Whyte's *Organization Man,* Erich Fromm's *Escape
from Freedom,* David Reisman's *Lonely Crowd,* spoke to the
nervousness about the consequences of Weberian rationalization, of mass culture and conformity, of alienation and
other-directedness. More radical voices such as those of C.
Wright Mills and Paul Goodman told of white-collar bu-
reaucrats and alienated youth with no outlets for their natural rebelliousness.

This undercoat of the Fifties reflects Daniel Bell's cultural
contradictions of capitalism. The official rhetoric of the society was increasingly hypocritical, glaringly out of sync with
actual behaviors, desires, and cues. Cultural traditionalism
tried to stop the seepage, but it was hopeless. Initially the
symptoms were contradictory and compromised, the sexuality of Jane Russell and Marilyn Monroe, the remarkable success of Hugh Hefner's *Playboy* with its call to consumer hedonism. But the main thrust of the booming consumer culture
was subversive, infinitely more so than the Beats or later the
hippies wrought. Television commercials selling cars, beer,
cigarettes; James Bond movies; Mickey Spillane novels; the
fascination with Frank Sinatra's rat pack and their antics—all
selling pleasure, marketing sex. As James Gilbert smartly concludes, much of the hysteria over juvenile delinquency during the 1950s reflected ambivalence about these mixed mes-
sages. Have fun, enjoy the good life, but be good. David and
Ricky Nelson, Bud and the other Anderson children never

strayed from the path of the good. But in the actual developing culture of abundance, the "bad" was very attractive.

The "bad" was sin, it was desire, it was sex. It was Marlon
Brando's *Wild Ones,* James Dean's *Rebel without a Cause;* it
was the young Elvis—teen hood; pink shirt, collar up, sleeves
rolled, Luckies in the fold; tight, pegged pants or Levis with
a stud belt. Elvis was every Harriet Nelson's nightmare—the
high school dropout, driving a truck, hanging out, becoming
those "white Negroes" Norman Mailer prefigured so brilliantly. The "bad" was one more time of whites putting to
their own use a romanticized vision of African American culture, on the wild side, down and dirty, dangerous, exciting.

Early rock 'n' roll, discovered by many white adolescents far
down on the radio dial—the black rhythm 'n' blues stations,
race music—was, in part, a rediscovery of the human body.
The rationalization of society, the turn toward corporate
niches and ticky-tacky suburbs, the buttoned-down, crew-cut,
narrow-tied, muted colors of the age of Ike and Mamie—all
this graying, this bundling, was a denial of those aspects of human existence that involved both the body and the soul, and
often the mind. Rock 'n' roll, following the legacies of the black
bottom, the Charleston, jazz, and swing, called forth a rebellion of the human animal, albeit at first in an adolescent, sing-
song manner. But the voice was loud and clear; rock, more
than jazz but similar to swing, was unequivocally dancing music, created to allow two people to simulate sex on a dance
floor, the devil's music indeed, as early moral-majority preach-
ers accurately contended. Woody Allen, very much a product
of the Fifties, once noted the best thing about sex was that it
was dirty. And "dirty dancing" was the next best thing.

This rebellion of the heart, of the body was part of a long-
term pushing of the envelope against nineteenth-century

Victorian repression. Warren Susman demonstrated the shift from a culture of character to one of personality as the United States, experiencing an organizational revolution, became defined by a new, white-collar middle class, a service economy. Leo Lowenthal showed how this transformation was marked by changes in the heroes and heroines of popular magazines, a movement from creators and producers, such as robber barons, inventors, military commanders, and industrial magnates, to consumers famous for their life-styles, such as athletes, movie stars. Whereas at one point people were admired for what they accomplished, as we moved into the culture of abundance, people were admired for what they consumed, for the pleasures that they enjoyed. We were well on the road to *People Magazine* and *The Lifestyles of the Rich and Famous* by the early twentieth century. Jay Gatsby, of course, is a key marker.

In the 1950s proper, the most prefiguring rebels were those of the beat generation, but resistance to modernization has many sources. In the United States, the traditionalist, southern *I'll Take My Stand* is one source; an assertion of culture over civilization, Lewis Mumford's life work defends scale, diversity, the idiosyncratic against the monumental, the cost-effective, the technocratic. Marshall Berman has brilliantly demonstrated how the Marxian tradition, Marx himself, is rooted in that part of the romantic tradition that generated Promethean, Faustian responses to industrial capitalism, to Blake's "dark satanic mills." But the bohemian tradition targeted the unsatisfactory culture created by the bourgeoisie, particularly the ways in which its materialist narrow-mindedness closed off aesthetic life springs, the possibilities of joy, of simplicity, of sensuality, of all matters creative except those under the domination of the cash nexus.

The beats of the postwar years were lineal descendants of those who created the Greenwich Village of the pre–World War I years, like Floyd Dell and Mabel Dodge Luhan, who spearheaded the assaults on Victorian morality.

Norman Mailer and Paul Goodman most insightfully captured the ways in which 1950s subterranean rebellions, especially that of the beats, prefigured what was to come in the Sixties. Mailer's "White Negro" essay embodied the sense of boredom among a sector of white, middle-class youth, restless in their newly constructed suburban homes, alienated from the compromises their successful parents seemed to have made, looking for some action, some signs of vitality, energy, meaning. As early as the 1920s, elite youth had found inspiration in their romantic versions of African American urban street life. They found a more relaxed, easy sense of the human body; a nonchalance about sexuality; a sense of the rhythms, as opposed to the geometry, of existence. And they were attracted to a Stagger Lee criminality, were thrilled with the dangers of a life that seemed to risk explosions of violence at any point and yet maintained a "cool," a mask of indifference in the face of ongoing risk.

Mailer translated these desires and fantasies and experimentations. He understood that the bohemian tradition valued experiment and experience, found bourgeois society, especially its U.S. version, most lacking in those qualities. His Reichian biases led him to identify with any life force rebelling against a carcinogenic culture, with the full stream of liberating energies blocked by, finally, sexual repression. Mailer imagined two directions, personified by Jack Kerouac and Allen Ginsberg, the gentile and the Jew, the athlete and the esthete. Mailer created psychological types, the hipster and the beatnik, the former seeking to fulfill the life of ex-

perimentation and full experience by extending out into the
world, through action, motion, "Go, man, go!"—sexual activity, drinkin', whorin', fightin'—the latter turning inward,
seeking to heighten consciousness by merging with the
whole, with God, with nature, shattering ego, desiring mys-
tical union through prayer, meditation, trance, hallucino-
genics. Mailer saw the psycho-logic of the hipster as an attraction to murder, to the Nietzschean transcendence of
human or God-based limitation. It was more compelling than
the ultimate orgasm; the ultimate experience, the transcendence of death by ordering it, arbitrarily, without petty material purpose—just to do it. On the other hand, the psycho-
logic of the beatnik, in obliterating the ego, was suicide, the
quest for nothingness, a numbness, an absence of feeling.

Mailer prefigured much of the downside of the 1960s
counterculture. Altamont, the flirtation with evil and violence, staged by Jagger and the Stones, enacted before their
bewildered, impotent eyes by the real thugs—the Hell's Angels; the fascination with and the celebration among Weath-
erpeople of Charles Manson are indicators, markers of the
ways in which the Romantic longing for ultimate experience,
its antinomian spirit led toward dangers, particularly when
countercultural visions were so enamored with the angelic
within our natures. The suicidal dimension (obviously part
of the drug culture at its worst) can be seen in the many
cultish surrenders by forlorn youth—to radical sects, to Je-
sus freaks, to Jim Jones and David Koresh.

Mailer recognized a longing out there that wasn't being addressed, not to speak of satisfied, by mainstream society. After all, perhaps the most telling measures of this dissatis-
faction came from government and elite sources. The Rock-
efeller brothers' reports of the late 1950s included *Prospect*

for America, which (paralleling much of Kennedy's generational rhetoric) expressed a certain nervousness about our future as a nation, as a civilization, not limited to the externalities of the Communist threat. Eisenhower's Commission on National Goals leads one to the problem: What's going on such that the most successful nation in human history, still in the midst of the golden age of its capitalist system, spreading middle-class prosperity to a widening circle of families, seems obsessed over, nervous about, uneasy over its very character, its raison d'être, its purposes? This is the heartland of what Holden Caulfield and James Dean and Elvis will mine.

This is the framework within which Jewish American story tellers—Malamud, Bellow, Philip Roth, and then Joseph Heller, but also Woody Allen, Sam Levinson, Mort Sahl, and Lenny Bruce—would teach Americans about how to cope within an existential alienation, how to beat oppressors and the fates to the punch with self-deprecating humor, how to find meaning in tragedy, nobility in vulgarity; how to be survivors. The other great exemplar was African American music and dance, particularly the blues. Two alien peoples, cultures, histories teaching mainstream Americans how to create culture out of pain, out of the cosmic joke. Both people of the Book, drawing lessons from a history of human suffering, from the burdens of oppression, from Job's lament. What would U.S. culture be without Jewish and black contributions? If only the Eisenhower consultants had understood how the quest for goals was already being transformed by Uncle Miltie and Little Richard.

Paul Goodman's *Growing Up Absurd* focused on the ways in which young people (especially, as with Mailer, males) were finding it tough to imagine an attractive path toward dulthood. Goodman was scathing in demonstrating how corporate violations of a sense of craft, such as built-in obsolescence and conformist bureaucratic culture, subverted the desires of young people to be productive and creative. He saw healthy patriotic urges undermined by McCarthyist demagogy and bipartisan mindlessness, sexual desires bottled up by a hypocritical culture, obsessed with brassieres, essentially telling its children, "Watch what I say, not what I do." It was a mentality of church on Sunday and screw your neighbor the rest of the week that Goodman, strongly empathizing with alienated youth, fixed upon.

Goodman also recognized the limitations of the options such alienated young people experienced, the "no exit" choices: delinquency, bohemianism, Old Left shibboleths, rat-race cynicism. To his credit, Goodman sought to articulate a position that valued the inherent patriotism, sense of honor, and interest in craft that he ascribed to young people.

It's of great significance, at least to me, more than thirty years after the book was written, after a generation of earth-shattering cultural challenge and rebellion, that (with the clear exception of Goodman's denigration of women's developmental dilemmas) *Growing Up Absurd* still sounds contemporary. The best of rock 'n' roll, from The Coasters to Pearl Jam, and most Hollywood movies about growing up—think of all the Brat Pack films—could cite *Growing Up Absurd*. Think of Neil Young's wonderful, neopunk screed, "Piece of Crap." One way of placing the 1960s in historical context is to recognize that what was experienced as alienating in the postwar years remains a relative constant as we enter the twenty-first century.

So as one approaches the 1960s, one feels a kind of nervous, anxious celebration, a neurotic chanting of "We're number one," a concern that perhaps the Pax Americana is to be short-lived, perhaps the seemingly vigorous, cocky Soviets are, in fact, finally, the future that really works. That's how one must read all of the *Life, Time, Look,* and *Reader's Digest* pieces on how Soviet schools, Soviet engineers, Soviet science were outperforming U.S. institutions. The boosterism of the 1950s, extensions of Depression-era yea-saying—the upbeat sermons of Norman Vincent Peale, the continuing influence of Dale Carnegie's *How to Win Friends and Influence People*—all contain a subtext of self-doubt and anxiety. The developing critique of Eisenhower in his second term—after the heart attacks, with the "loss" of Cuba, with the near disaster of Nixon in Venezuela, with the humiliating U-2 capture—was a variant on a "decline of Rome" metaphor. We were old, like Ike; the Soviets were somehow youthful . . . like, who? Khrushchev? Perhaps more like their showcased Olympic athletes and their celebrated cosmonauts (Yuri Gagarin: "I am eagle!").

As we approached the Kennedy years, driven in part by a strenuous effort to counter this fear about decline, one must recall the literature of the late Fifties, bemoaning the apathy of youth, the silence of a generation, its greater interest in retirement plans than in risk taking. The Soviets, who were outsmarting us diplomatically, according to the best-selling *Ugly American,* were more entrepreneurial as well! It was American youth who seemed to be bland, conformist, seeking only to fit into some corporate niche. And our best intellectuals were only slightly uncomfortable with an end to ideology, an apparent closing off of utopian dreams, an anxious belief that Keynesian fine tuning and attacks on tail fins and TV wastelands would fend off Weberian nightmares of spiritual bankruptcy.

3

New Left, New Right, New World

As Daniel Bell anticipated an end of ideology, as Louis Hartz concluded that there was only a liberal tradition in America, as most social scientists assumed the inevitability of a modernization process that peaked with the mature welfare state, as Kenneth Keniston worried about the apathy of educated youth, we entered the 1960s.

At that moment not only did virtually no observer anticipate the coming of a radical upsurge, but if any activism was expected it was assumed to be of the Right rather than of the Left. Dan Wakefield, in his memoir *New York in the Fifties,* recalls that the early Goldwater boom led him to assume that "the conservative boomlet on campuses was a rising tide that would define the Sixties generation." And Murray Kempton, in 1962, proclaimed, "We must assume that the conservative revival is *the* youth movement of the sixties." Wakefield even projected that the

Goldwater youth movement might be "as important to its epoch as the Young Communist League was to the thirties" (265–270).

So, what happened, and why did it happen? What accounts for the rise of *any* significant ideological youth movement during the 1960s? And what accounts for the seeming primacy of a leftward rather than a rightward one? A culture that seemed to be on a very stable track toward a Keynesian mixed economy got on a roller coaster ride that includes destabilizers as diverse as Abbie Hoffman, George Wallace, Barry Goldwater, Huey Newton, Robin Morgan, Ken Kesey, Tim Leary, Bella Abzug, Tom Hayden, and Bob Dylan.

One way to begin to figure out how permanence turned into change is to examine how particular groups imagined the engines of such change. For example, what distinguishes beats from hippies is that the former never anticipated social change; their very beatness rested on a sense of the hopelessness of penetrating the suburban walls of the new bourgeoisie. All that was left to do was to howl at the injustices and to build countercommunities of the blessed in the enclaves of Greenwich Village, North Beach, and other less populous but sympatico places. The beats embraced jazz, increasingly a highly specialized, sophisticated music that, at one extreme, was literally turning its back on its audiences. They were contemptuous of mass culture, bubble-gum rock 'n' roll or Patti Page pop. They were in the classical mold of the romantic, bohemian tradition, almost needing the dull, repressed middle class to juxtapose with their quest for a life of the ultimate experiences, the experimental life. Their heroes were those who burnt the candle at both ends, tested the limits of consciousness, of experience itself, internal or external.

It must have been strikingly clear that the cultural contradictions of 1950s capitalism were stretched to the breaking point. The beats were, in some ways, merely the low-cost version of what Hugh Hefner was marketing for a faster lane of consumption. In *The Hearts of Men*, Barbara Ehrenreich shrewdly concludes that men were moving toward a new version of the double standard, based on sexual access. She suggests that beats and playboys were variants of a common flight from the responsibilities of marriage and family. Why should the *Playboy* reader, now having available disposable income, now living in an environment that promoted the titillation of pleasures, give up the fullest range of sexual possibilities? Why hand over one's hard-earned income to a wife? Why sacrifice the same for children? The beat version argued that the kind of effort involved in earning that hefty disposable income was unnecessary to achieve the same, even greater, pleasure. Drop the wall-to-wall carpeting, the sporty Corvette and the expensive suits, the insurance and the home mortgage; instead, simplify, simplify, simplify! With a pad, a mattress, enough to maintain the essentials of books and records, one could concentrate on what really matters—beauty, truth, pleasure. Ya' can't be a free man on weekends if you're a corporate slave Mondays through Fridays. Women were welcomed into this club, but all too often the beat men were not prepared to grant them the same privileges. It was a cushy deal; the men got liberated from the responsibilities of family. And they were heroic.

Social change requires an anticipation of the heroic. The beats limited their anticipation to individual and small-group acts—the Kerouac hero on the road, always in motion, ready for balling and brawling; the brilliant jazz readings of Ginsberg or Gregory Corso, stretching the language, reviving the oral tradition. Their hero was one who could shock the bourgeoisie, "freak them out," as the term developed later; but there was no belief in changing society, in making history, not even the desire to. After all, in an era of Stanley Kowalski, the first Polish joke, of Ralph Kramden as working-class stiff, of Ozzie and Harriet and David and Ricky, where might one invest hope?

Many of the beats, like their predecessors of the 1920s, did invest in African American street life—sexuality, drugs, jazz, crime, cool. But this was simply part of the counterculture's attempt to integrate into Bohemia all of the anti-Wests—Zen Buddhism, Navaho, Mayan, gypsy, Hindu, Taoist, outlaw, psychopath, insane. Only with the countercultural hippies of the 1960s would come an expectation that the heroes of experience and experiment might be the pied pipers of suburban youth, stealing children away from their uptight parents with the holy trinity of sex, drugs, and rock 'n' roll. Abbie Hoffman and Jerry Rubin, the yippies, would be the first to anticipate the possibilities of a Woodstock Nation, a greening of America. The rock world would toss out and then destroy some of the pied pipers, Jim Morrison most particularly.

This aspect of the 1960s rests on a recognition that the culture needed some liberating, needed to soften the contradictions between its pleasure-driven economy and its Victorian and quite ambivalent codes. Godfrey Hodgson emphasized how the counterculture, despite itself, played into the functional need of a mass production, culture-of-abundance economy to market mass consumption, credit-card buying, what Stuart Ewen calls "the psychic desire to consume."

It is as if the culture jumped from super-ego controls to id impulses without passing through or gaining very much ego strength. We went from denial of bodily pleasures to moral imperatives to fuck. Obsession, as Calvin Klein must understand, remained a constant. The consequences were invaluable, if fraught with disasters and long-term problems. As the quest for a heroic agency of social change collapsed under the weight of Altamont and, perhaps more significantly, the downturn of the economy, the counterculture was reduced to merely partying, to a routinizing of greater degrees of sexual and linguistic freedoms, wider ranges of life-style choices, greater tolerance for deviances. The limitations were noted by Michael Harrington in a thoughtful essay on the decline of Bohemia. When the middle class buys into pleasure and cheers and encourages the avant-garde cultural rebels—in fact, gets off on being freaked out, *longs* to be freaked out, and pays big bucks to be freaked out—Bohemia is subverted.

Whereas the bohemians, beat and hippie, used negritude as a means toward their own liberation from Wasp repressiveness, those more traditionally left of center, especially the New Left, found another kind of inspiration in black America. Here is the beginning, the alpha, the source of the rise of a New Left, of all the social movements of the 1960s. In fact, what we mean by the Sixties begins with the civil rights revolution.

This is not particularly controversial, but it cannot be overemphasized. In a climate without expectations, with an increasingly comfortable unionized working class, with Khrushchev's Twentieth Party Congress denunciation of Stalin's crimes, with only existential commitments seemingly available, the civil rights revolution inspired that segment of educated youth who would form the New Left.

Many of the first cohort of New Leftists were from liberal homes with core liberal values; they were disproportionately Jewish, prone to identify with the underdog. But even in such cases there were alternatives to creating a new radical student movement. Tom Hayden, a Catholic growing up in suburban Royal Oak, aspiring to be an international correspondent, a heroic journalist, found initial inspiration in the cultural rebellions associated with *Catcher in the Rye,* with James Dean, with Kerouac's *On the Road.* He took to the road, to Berkeley, where he found civil rights with a little help from his new friends. The experience of going south was a catalyst for many of the founding members of Students for a Democratic Society. They saw southern blacks behaving with great dignity in the face of White Citizens Council terrorism; they sat in churches rocking with a religious enthusiasm and a sense of community few had experienced in their northern, college-educated families. From such experiences, they came to view themselves as a political elite—although they would have blanched at the terminology—interested in enriching individual lives through commitment to the creation of a beloved community. As James Miller has noted, this belief in a participatory democracy was laced with contradictory desires: one, to construct pure, thoroughly egalitarian and liberated lives; two, to extend such lives to all oppressed and marginalized people. The former tended to lead to an enclave model within which one first liberated oneself in a communal setting, purifying oneself to earn the validity, the sanctification, to change others. The latter desire led to bringing the revolution to the masses; those masses, at first the southern blacks, were expanded to what early SDS called "an interracial movement of the poor."

To early SDS and the New Left, the agent of social change was youth itself, heroic youth, the hero as revolutionary activist. As long as there was a belief that "out there" was a constituency—sharecroppers, the unemployed, students, freaks,

Third World peoples—this model had resiliency. It began with the fifty thousand African Americans of Montgomery, Alabama, refusing to ride the segregated buses; its last gasp included the Black Panthers and the Viet Cong.

Recall that when the 1960s began virtually no one, except perhaps C. Wright Mills, anticipated that there would be a New Left of young intelligentsia. The hero of the moment seemed to be a witty, stylish Cold Warrior, John Fitzgerald Kennedy. Norman Mailer, in his idiosyncratic fashion, understood the heroic possibilities in Kennedy, a bringing together of the aphrodesiac of Washington power, Hollywood and Broadway glamour, and Cambridge gray matter. Kennedy seemed to be all that Eisenhower was *not:* young, energetic, risk taking, hatless, sexy, articulate. Perhaps the empire was not in decline; perhaps the young prince could turn things about, establish Camelot.

The Sixties began with the election of Kennedy. And the response to Kennedy, especially among intellectuals and artists, among the growing educated professional middle classes (granted their preference for the patrician Stevenson) reflected a desire to escape the Weberian cage, to find ways to halt the erosion of imagination and creativity and spontaneity. My favorite movie of that period is Herb Gardner's *A Thousand Clowns,* in which a free spirit—harassed by Chuckles the Clown and his mindless morning TV show, worn down by a heartless state bureaucracy that refuses to see that, despite his joblessness, despite his essential irresponsibility about parenting and housekeeping, he is trying desperately to raise his nephew, Nick—marches off to his gray-flannel, buttoned-down, white-collar job. He surrenders. What were his options in the America before the Sixties? He joined Paul Goodman's cynical rat race after at least giving the system a goose and a ride.

Whereas the New Left was inspired by the civil rights revolution, by the heroism of African Americans, those who created the New Right seemed driven by their resistance to the very same. What drove the conservative surge on campuses that Dan Wakefield and Murray Kempton anticipated during Kennedy's thousand days?

The standard accounts of the rise of conservatism in the 1950s emphasize the role of fusionism in balancing the contradictions that had limited conservative unity up to that moment. Prior to the emergence of William F. Buckley, Jr.'s *National Review,* conservatism seemed destined for the ideological scrap heap, another victim of the inexorable triumph of the welfare state. There wasn't even agreement about the use of the term *conservative* to describe an alternative to the ongoing liberal consensus. On one hand the free-market libertarianism of Friedrich Hayek and his circle argued that all forms of state intervention, in circumscribing individual liberties associated with the marketplace, tended toward totalitarianism. On the other hand various forms of traditionalist ideologies, rooted in Edmund Burke and Joseph de Maistre, focused on the value of an organic community, sometimes idealized as medieval, sometimes as agrarian southern, but always suspicious of the Enlightenment privileging of reason. If the libertarian strand worshiped liberty, the traditionalist segment was devoted to community. Foremost, there was the issue of anti-Communism, seized by the fusionists, to produce the awkward coalition of Adam Smith and Edmund Burke.

As opposed to the counterculture and the New Left, conservatism was not distinctively a youth movement. Buckley's *National Review* drew on mostly experienced veterans of the ideological wars of the New Deal and McCarthy period—

ex-Communists turned anti-Communists, conservative Catholic intellectuals, free marketeers. What interests me is the idealism, the ways in which this developing conservatism, analogous to New Left radicalism, saw itself as a moral challenge to the welfare state. After all, the Politics of Growth was at the top of its game when Buckley launched his journal or even when the Young Americans for Freedom adopted the Sharon Statement at Buckley's Connecticut estate several months before Kennedy edged Nixon out for the presidency in 1960.

In that election, both candidates stood for variants of the liberal consensus. They were anti-ideological moderates, both ferocious but pragmatic anti-Communists in foreign policy, both comfortable with maintaining and incrementally expanding the welfare state. Only one, however—Kennedy—was in the heroic mold, with his generational appeal, his forceful and eloquent call for national service in the form of the Peace Corps and the Green Berets. But even Kennedy was most of all a technician, a fine tuner of an already rationalized, functional system.

But on both the Left and Right, challenges commenced that would have profound impact on the body politic, that would shake and shatter operating assumptions about the nature and direction of modernization. Historians need to explore and analyze the ways in which these two challenges formed and expressed themselves, what they had in common and how they differed. It seems clear to me that the politics of the late 1990s, as E. J. Dionne, Jr., has so powerfully noted, are being driven by both the successes and the ultimate inadequacies of those challenges to the welfare state raised by the New Right and New Left.

The New Right, as suggested earlier, was adult initiated.

Buckley and then the Goldwater movement were the primary energizers. However it seems to me that a battle for cultural hegemony occurred on college campuses in the late 1950s and throughout the 1960s; while most college youth were attempting, not always successfully, to get on with making lives and careers and families, small but fervent aspiring elites were imagining the making of history.

The Fifties postwar culture offered significant possibilities to intellectually driven students. In the midst of the cultural wasteland of TV and suburbia was a vibrant, attractive culture in the making. New York intellectuals were carving out major spaces in our institutional, cultural life; New York replaced Paris as the capital of the world of art; *Commentary, Partisan Review,* the *New Yorker* brought the most stimulating of an increasingly global culture to those interested in an alternative to the corporate rat race. It would be most unwise to underestimate the vibrancy of Fifties elite culture and its academic aspects.

Within that academy, the dominant voices in the humanities were those valuing notions of paradox, ambiguity, tragedy, while in the social sciences structural-functionalism reigned. It wasn't a friendly environment for bohemian poets, Marxists, or conservatives attracted to the writings of Richard Weaver or Russell Kirk. A liberalism of "the vital center" was in the saddle.

The conservative challenge on campuses seems to have attracted a different audience than would the New Left movement. The New Left students were more affluent, more likely to be Jewish or from secular Protestant denominations and to attend elite institutions than those who joined the Goldwater student movement. Conservative youth were more likely to be Catholic, middle class, and attending second-level institutions. What were they thinking? What attracted them to conservatism?

The Sharon Statement is one way to begin an answer, especially when one considers it in light of the more well known Port Huron Statement of SDS. It presupposes, as did Kennedy and SDS, a "time of moral and political crisis." SDS saw a crisis in the contradictions between U.S. ideals and U.S. performance in a context darkened by the cloud of nuclear annihilation. To YAFers, the crisis was as Kennedy defined it: "The forces of international Communism are, at present, the greatest single threat to" our liberties. But the young conservatives differed from Kennedy both in their assessment of how to engage that global threat and in how domestic forces impacted on our capacity to triumph. It's interesting to contrast the sense of generational identity of Port Huron ("We are people of this generation, bred in at least modest comfort, housed now in universities, looking uncomfortably to the world we inherit.") with that of YAF, who took a more traditional, ideological approach to manifesto writing. YAFers exhibited no sign of introspective concerns.

SDS pinpoints the fight against Jim Crow and racism, the alienation of "meaningless work," and the contrast between "superfluous abundance" and global poverty; SDSers set their generational moment in the decline of colonialism and in the zero-sum terror of the Cold War. There's, indeed, nothing about considering themselves as did the first SDSers, as possibly "the last generation in the experiment with living" in the Sharon Statement. Although the words don't appear in the statement, they clearly would "rather be dead than red." YAF idealism begins with "eternal truths" and "transcendent values." YAFers' communal desires rest on such universals, but the zeal of the document is for freedom, their own version of what SNCC called a "freedom high." In this case it is driven by God's providence, a "right to be free from the restrictions of arbitrary force," to experience a liberty that is "indivisible," that is, resting on economic and political freedom. The communal, traditionalist dimension returns to restrict government, to protect these freedoms "through the preservation of internal order, the provision of national defense, and the administration of justice." Conservative youth stood for what would soon be called law and order, maximum defense spending, and a willingness to have that very same government violate individual rights under the primacy of national security needs.

The Sharon Statement goes on to invest these rights to liberty in the YAF version of constitutional law, most especially in a states' rights stance vis-à-vis federal tyrannies and in a veneration for the invisible hand of the market.

The attractions of this manifesto are clear. The Soviet Union embodied evil and was aggressively pursuing its interests in the world. We needed to confront that aggression with all our resources. There was a moral fervor in denying any accommodation in our relations with the Soviets. How could one compromise with Stalinists and their heirs? Why not seek victory, as both the Sharon Statement and Barry Goldwater, in his campaign writings, demanded?

Liberals, including ferocious anti-Communists like Kennedy, held to what I call pragmatic anti-Communism. They saw Communism as evil, but recognized that it existed within historical, geographical entities called nation-states, which had interests that were more finite, less cosmic. Conservatives held to a strictly ideological version of anti-Communism. It was seamless, demonic, absolute. There were only "the" Communists, not the variations that many liberals, at least in private, increasingly recognized, for instance, Soviet versus Chinese Communists; Yugoslavian Communism; Western European, "polycentric" Communism, and so on. Whereas the liberals saw a long-term protracted struggle along a series of fault lines, which required a vigilant containment against Communist expansion, the Goldwaterite conservatives saw an avaricious enemy taking advantage of a morally weak, half-socialistic West.

What the conservatives had more difficulty in addressing was the North-South fault rooted in decolonization. For the most part they were fighting the tide of history, aligning themselves with colonial rulers, with South African apartheid, with every Third World dictator who mouthed an anti-Communist line. Of course, the liberals were not far behind, often afraid to open themselves up to neo-McCarthyite assaults. But the liberals—Kennedy, for example—had more confidence, were more in touch with historical trends. Kennedy saw himself in a global, moral rivalry with an upstart Communism; he understood that the United States was in a contest for the hearts and minds of Third World people and that the country couldn't simply stand for the status quo or, worse, the colonial past. Buckley's *National Review* too often seemed to prefer the British Colonial Office to a genuine self-determination of all nations. The conservative position in foreign affairs did project idealism, but this was marred by its tendency toward nostalgia for the ancient regimes and contempt for Third World peoples that finally rested on racism.

By its nature, campus conservatism could attract some idealists to its foreign policy militancy but suffered from its racial parochialisms, its snobberies. Second-generation Catholic youth might find inspiration in an ideological anti-Communism directed against Iron Curtain domination, but there was this *National Review* racial snobbery to manage. Many couldn't.

On college campuses, many emerging conservative students were inspired by the novels and objectivist philosophy of Ayn Rand. *The Fountainhead* and *Atlas Shrugged* were campus best-sellers; they offered a heroic alternative to the vital center, a laissez-faire libertarianism ferocious in its opposition to state powers. In many ways, Rand cuts to the heart of what drove much of New Right idealism—its association with the frontier individualism in American mythology. What if those of us who are the true creators withdrew our services from the parasites? Why can't a creator destroy what others have stolen from him? Here was a muscular option to Adlai Stevenson and the grandfatherly Ike!

Ayn Rand's dilemma was that she was an Enlightenment devotee, a prophet of reason, an adversary of sentimentality, most especially all forms of religion. To Rand, religion was a measure of cowardice, an evasion of the material realities. She was truly a nineteenth-century Manchester liberal and, of course, an incurable romantic. For this reason, she and her movement could not fuse—in fact, constantly defused. Objectivism denied the truths of what Peter Clecak calls "temperamental conservatism" and "philosophical conservatism." The former rests on a congenital caution: "If it ain't broke, don't fix it." the latter, more powerfully—articulated by Kirk, Robert Nisbet, Richard Weaver, Peter Viereck, rooted in traditions that begin with Edmund Burke—saw religious, moral authority as essential to the stability of all social orders. These cultural conservatives couldn't abide Rand's mix of rationalism and romanticism; they held firmly to a belief in human frailty, in sin itself. Both tended toward an acceptance of human inequality, but Rand's celebration of selfishness, of the lack of any responsibilities toward others, contrasted with cultural conservatism's belief that those more able and fortunate had social responsibilities toward their "inferiors." Rand's militant atheism, finally, ruled her out as a part of *National Review* fusionism, but her single-minded individualism inspired many who joined the developing New Right.

It would be fascinating to know how many Ayn Rand devotees ended up as New Left or countercultural rebels. There clearly has been movement from right to left (Karl Hess and Garry Wills are the most notable examples) and from left to right (the second thoughts examples of Peter Collier and David Horowitz come to mind); there have also been figures like Murray Rothbard, whose libertarianism led him to significantly ally himself with the New Left despite his free-market ideology. Right or Left?

The New Left dominated the 1960s social movements because it understood and proceeded to act on the need to reconcile U.S. promise with U.S. performance. The New Left *begins* with its recognition of the centrality of the civil rights revolution. And the radical movements of the 1960s play a catalytic role in the expansion of democratic rights to a wider and wider set of Americans, beginning with African Americans and extending to women, Hispanics, Native Americans, the disabled, gays and lesbians, and, by force of example, ethnic Americans. The de-Waspization of America was accomplished as the promise of our historical mandate—"All men are created equal"—was extended to all previously marginalized, oppressed groups.

Influenced by the bohemian tradition and intertwined with the counterculture, the New Left also recognized that there needed to be more freedom for all peoples to express themselves. While the conceit that fucking in the streets while high on acid and grooving to rock 'n' roll would make people revolutionary proved to be illusory, the cultural and political rebellions of the Sixties did lead to more choice, more tolerance, more spontaneity and flair. We have become a significantly more diverse culture with what began as a "Black is beautiful" campaign.

The New Left developed a concept of corporate liberalism, a critique of the developing welfare state, that was of two minds. On the one hand, it criticized the incompleteness and therefore the hypocrisies of the U.S. welfare state. It saw and attacked racism and poverty, soon to be joined by sexism, homophobia, and other forms of exclusion. But the New Left, at its very heart, did not believe that the system had the capacity to reach completeness; the New Left's heart was socialist. It doubted the capacity of capitalism to achieve its utopian dreams of middle classlessness, what Lyndon Johnson called the Great Society, which in part was to be the consequence of the War on Poverty and a wide assortment of other Politics-of-Growth programs. On the other hand, New Leftists called into question the attractiveness of such an accomplishment. The argument that the very *success* of the system, its ability to deliver the goods, its suburban soul, was defective and unworthy of liberated citizens in fact drove much of the New Left's vision. It was the *successful* welfare state that New Leftists attacked; such an entity risked the fulfillment of the Weberian nightmare of soullessness, because it was technocratic, antidemocratic, elitist, culturally degrading, philistine, alienating. Alienation was the sine qua non of critique. Capitalism, in encouraging competition, in requiring a restless acquisitiveness, fell short of addressing the human potential to experience a more participatory community based on authentic values, such as pleasure, beauty, truth, unalienating work.

The New Left would remain ambivalent about the welfare state throughout its brief history. Tom Hayden's romance with Robert Kennedy, precisely at the point at which he is becoming a romantic communist, reflects this ambivalence. An attraction to the heroics of the Kennedys, especially Bobby's more populist, visceral style, his existential, Irish, passionate, touching politics, indicate ways in which the New Left focused on a critique of a rationalized, bureaucratic welfare state. There was something *missing* from the vital center—vitality itself.

That the New Right was behind the historical curve on a number of issues explains its lesser successes during the 1960s. YAF and other conservative youth organizations, the Goldwater campaign—all resisted, to their shame, the truths of the civil rights revolution. Under the guise of states' rights, they exploited racist bigotries and contradicted their own commitments to a libertarian belief in equal opportunity and a traditionalist commitment to gradual change. They stood for no change at all, other than the rollback of both Communism and the liberal welfare state.

And while campus conservatives were part of the early Free Speech Movement, as they had been part of the deviant subculture of Greenwich Village of the early 1960s, their libertarian voice was drowned out by their more elitist desires. Campus conservatives were mostly enamored with Bill Buckley's style, his wit, his vocabulary; he was the role model. And it was an aristocratic one; attractive to working-class and middle-class youth seeking their own way toward respectability, toward the accoutrements of culture. And Buckley personified—despite what many of his ideological foes note to be his personal decency and humanity—the still-reactionary qualities of conservatism: its tendency to admire Third World thugs, its jokes about wogs, its snobbery.

What needed to happen for the New Right to effectively compete with the New Left for a leadership role in making challenges to the welfare state was a shift from Buckley Anglophilia to alternative populism. Tom and Mary Edsall and E. J. Dionne tell us, in great detail, how conservatives made this very successful shift. They had available the excesses of the New Left: a developing radical elitism, an anti-Americanism, a patronizing support for oppressed groups no matter the validity of the claim, a radically antinomian tolerance for behaviors that contributed to the breakdown of law and order.

New Right conservatives only needed the breaking down of the welfare state, the economic crises that halted the growth upon which the Politics of Growth relied, to envision and act upon a more populist political strategy. The people those Buckleyites had viewed with a kind of archcontempt might be open to conservative arguments, after all. Goldwater, then George Wallace, Governor Ronald Reagan, then Richard Nixon and Spiro Agnew—all demonstrated the ways in which a great silent majority of Middle Americans, ethnics, hard hats, Archie Bunkers, Bubbas and good ol' boys, fundamentalists and evangelicals resented and opposed what conservatives called the new "special interests," articulated by a "new class" of "pointy-headed intellectuals," "nattering nabobs of negativity." Nixon called them "bums."

The New Left had been built, despite its ambivalences, on traditional liberal, Democratic visions of "the people" against "the interests." Liberalism and varieties of socialism always have shared an inherent suspiciousness of the capacity of capitalists to pursue the public interest and a belief that the pursuit of profit was a problematical moral goal.

The New Right, on the other hand, celebrated that pursuit

and had an alternative suspiciousness concerning the benevolence of all state activities but for those related to defense, police, and morality. When the liberal consensus fell apart and the New Left and related movements fragmented into a politics of group identity, there was room for a conservative resurgence. The New Right could now engage in its own assaults on the welfare state in the belief that free markets and competition would open up greater areas for human liberty.

From the vantage point of the 1990s one can argue that both New Left and New Right—and neobohemian—critiques had cogent arguments about the inadequacies of the vital center. The neobohemians, the hippies and freaks, would provoke the culture toward greater tolerance for difference and greater capacity for human pleasure. They would also force all of us to pay more attention to the ways we treated our bodies and the earth itself. It was not a marginal contribution to help Americans see that knowledge without wisdom, work without play, sex without pleasure, religion without spirituality were unsatisfactory.

The New Left clearly would contribute much that would fundamentally change our society for the better, especially in extending rights and opportunities to previously excluded groups. It also played a major role by challenging mindless anti-Communist approaches to the Cold War in opposing our military interventions in Indochina.

The New Right reminded many of us that there was life in conservatism after all. While conservatives often took the low road toward exclusion, bigotry, and a kind of "I've got mine" selfishness, they also forced all parties to consider the repressive, manipulative, and life-inhibiting qualities of the state; they reopened the issue of the value of the marketplace in democratic decision making. This alone was an invaluable contribution, given that both liberal and socialist traditions had tended to increasingly privilege state interventions, particularly in the economy. As an issue of liberty, this had to be, finally, compelling to liberals and democratically inclined radicals.

In addition, conservatives forced all parties to come to grips with the ways in which the New Left notions of empowerment and participatory democracy could not be limited to particular groups but had to extend to what they called Middle Americans. Or else. Those who would move past Buckley's polysyllables and eschew Wallace's pitches to bigotry would invest conservative values in a new politics of "the people" against "the special interests," the producing classes of Kevin Phillips against the parasitic alliance of new-class intellectuals and welfare cheats and criminals. Their moment in the political sun would come after the radical movements of the Sixties lost their sense of direction.

Vietnam: Silent-Majority
Baby Boomers

In James Fallows's "What Did You Do in the Class War, Daddy?" Harvard antiwar activists, mostly exempt from the war through student deferments or psychiatric rationalizations submitted by friendly shrinks, look on as sons of Cambridge blue-collar workers march off to boot camp. The imagery is powerful and, as I shall suggest, deceptive. In our images of the generation who lived through the Vietnam era, we tend toward a dualism of doves and vets, the soon-to-be-yuppie twentysomethings and the victimized salt-of-the-earth GIs of Oliver Stone's *Platoon*. The Sixties generation is divided into those who served their country and those who opposed its policies. And it follows that those who opposed the war from the safety of the class-privileged deferments and evasions lose the moral high ground, in fact, face the charge of hypocrisy and cowardice.

However, there is a sizable group among the Sixties

generation whose experience fits neither that of activist doves nor that of blue-collar vets. Lawrence M. Baskir and William A. Strauss describe, in *Chance and Circumstance: The Draft, the War, and the Vietnam Generation,* the demographic characteristics of baby-boom males. Twenty-seven million men became eligible for the draft in the period between the Gulf of Tonkin Resolution of August 1964 and the withdrawal of the last military forces from Indochina in March 1973. Of these men, 8.6 million served in the military during the Vietnam period, 2,850,000 in Southeast Asia, 2,150,000 actually in Vietnam. This leaves more than 18 million draft-age men who did not serve in the military, and 26 million women. Given even the largest of the estimated sizes of the antiwar movement, the number of active protesters could have formed no more than 20 percent (10.6 million) of the total population of the generation. Indeed, a 1973 study by John Mueller shows that "those *under* thirty consistently supported the war in larger percentages than those over thirty."

One may reasonably conclude that of the 53 million members of the baby-boom generation who did not serve in Vietnam, a majority were neither activists nor in possession of any strong sentiments against the war. In addition to those who protested and those who served (and in significant proportions also protested), a third contingent must be highlighted—those who were part of the silent majority of baby boomers. Such people, whatever their feelings about the war, rarely engaged in any organized opposition and, at the same time, made conscious efforts to minimize the possibility of finding themselves on the battlefield. In sum, most of those who benefited from their social-class privileges were not antiwar protesters. Most, in fact, stood on the sidelines as some went off to fight and others marched in opposition.

The three suburban towns of southern New Jersey that I have studied reflect this third possibility and stand as such a silent majority. These three towns, totaling about twenty thousand people in the mid-Sixties, were among the most affluent within a then economically struggling and still semi-rural county. For example, the towns ranked second, fourth, and thirteenth in median family income within Atlantic County; the wealthiest town's income was virtually double that of impoverished Atlantic City, ranked twenty-fourth. The residents of the three towns were solid, middle-class, white Americans. Virtually all were Christian, about 70 percent Protestant, 30 percent Catholic. Almost three-quarters voted Republican.

The graduating class of 1966 at the local high school includes 129 males. I have been able to track 102 of them. No one from the class of 1966 died in Vietnam, and I have found only five who served there, including one at a Thai air base and another off the coast on an aircraft carrier. In fact, no graduates from any class died in Vietnam; one local resident died there in 1962, but he was born in 1930 and consequently went to high school before the new regional school existed.

It's of some value to compare this experience in Vietnam with that of less affluent, more minority-based communities. Atlantic City, for example, with approximately twice the population, lost 16 young men; next-door Pleasantville, with two-thirds the population, lost 7. The large ghettoized city of Newark contributed 111 of New Jersey's total of 1,480 Vietnam War deaths. Edison High School, a mostly Latino and African American institution located in the North Philadelphia ghetto, lost 54 students to the war. Indeed, the inequities of the draft guaranteed that the Vietnam War would have most impact on working-class, poor, and minority communities.

The South Jersey area was decidedly hawkish and conventionally anti-Communist. Many of its baby boomers had dads who had served in World War II or Korea. Pro-military feelings were reinforced by the families' working at NAFEC (National Aviation Facilities Experimental Center), particularly those associated with the 177th Tactical Fighter Group stationed there. Families valued patriotism, flying the flag on appropriate holidays and coming out to commemorate service and sacrifice during holidays like the Fourth of July. They were disposed to accept the words of one mayor, spoken at the 1966 Memorial Day services: "We are demonstrating our reverence for those who shed their life's blood defending our nation's freedom." The mayor posited that Vietnam was "a critical test of the so-called wars of liberation as instigated by Communism." His declaration that retreat from Vietnam would "be catastrophic to peoples throughout the world who are working to achieve their independence" was well within the ideological framework of most local residents.

The year 1966 was the first in which the Vietnam War was likely to impose itself on graduates of the high school. The class of 1965 received their diplomas before Johnson's "best and brightest" confirmed and put into motion troop commitments of close to two hundred thousand by the end of the year. War was in the air, but graduates still weren't feeling the heat. By June 1966, the war's pressure on the draft was apparent. It is striking how few graduates answered the call. At least upon reflection, many speak of resistance to marching off to war. Something seemed awry—this wasn't a declared war; it was off somewhere outside the students' focus of attention or knowledge. They listened to their history and civics teachers, often veterans, evoke Cold War shibboleths, but somehow it all seemed remote, alien, at least until their senior year. Of the twenty-five males I interviewed, ten were deferred from service because of injury, school, or lottery number. Twelve men served in the reserve or National Guard units: six in the navy reserve, two in the Air National Guard, and one in the Coast Guard. Only four went into the army, two of whom served the standard one-year tour in Vietnam, although neither in combat situations. One of the naval reservists, while on active duty, served a tour aboard the USS *Ticonderoga,* a carrier whose bombers struck enemy targets from the Gulf of Tonkin. For most 1966 grads, Vietnam remained at some distance; many spoke, in the 1980s, of knowing no Vietnam veterans, knowing no one who was killed or seriously wounded over there.

Bobby Green, describing Vietnam as "a poor man's war," tells of several dropouts who served in combat. Bobby remembers being in high school when Timmy Aker came back to tell war stories of his marine tour in Vietnam: "Timmy was a tough kid. Every other word he used when he was young was 'motherfucker,' m.f. this and m.f. that; he had a real neat style about him, a little bit wild. Well, he quit school, and he joined the marines, and all of a sudden Vietnam was starting to make the news, and Timmy's over there. All of a sudden, boom! Timmy's back, Purple Heart; something happened and a mine got tripped, couple of people got killed, and he survived it—now he's out. We're out in the woods drinking, and Timmy would come, and he could take twenty, thirty guys, and we'd all stand around, and he would talk, tell stories, and we'd laugh, listening to him talk about his experiences over there. Now it's starting to come to us." To Bobby and his mostly lower-middle- and working-class buddies, "it was the America kick-ass kind of thing; it was a skirmish still at that time." Bobby recalls when a book on the Green Berets came out: "Joey Campion's wife's brother, whose name was Vic Wills, he read the book, and he was telling us one night [reading from the book], 'And he came running over the hill and grabbed some gook by the neck and ripped it out by his mouth, and the blood and the killing and all that'—wow!"

Bobby and his rowdy friends were patriotic, even gung ho, but still wanted to enjoy the summer before joining up: "We used to go almost every day down to the marine recruiter in Atlantic City and sit and talk to him, and he kept saying, 'You got to go for four years,' and we'd say, 'No, that's too long.' Timmy Aker used to say, 'Don't go for four years; go for two. And if you find out you like it, you can always re-up.' That made sense to me, 'cause I know how I am with authority and regimentation; I love to play football, but I hated to practice." So this rowdy crowd of guys kept talking with the recruiters: "We used to ask stupid questions: 'When we're out in the field, will you bring us cold beer?' 'Oh, yeah, we'll bring you beer.' Then about a month after, our apartment got raided for underage drinking. Got our names in the papers, the whole bit." Several guys immediately took the four-year marine enlistment, but Bobby resisted. In early 1968 he got his draft notice. At the time, Bobby Green knew no one who either opposed or was involved in protesting against the war. "It was still 'Yah, we'll kick ass and we'll win the war' and all that." The campus demonstrations "weren't affecting us here." Bobby couldn't have found Vietnam on a map at that point. The network news and newspaper headlines may have been highlighting "the armies of the night," the campus rallies against the draft, the Students for a Democratic Society (SDS), but on the Coast such news was at best distant and more typically ignored.

Al Judson concurs; like most 1966 graduates, he knew

next to nothing about Vietnam: "I don't remember talking about it in high school." College-bound, more middle-class students like Judson had less interest in the war than Bobby Green and his academically bored buddies. They assumed that four years of college would protect them; of course, this war against a backward Third World country couldn't go on for that long. Harry Kearns says that he had vague knowledge of the war, but mostly, "I knew the Communists were trying to take over and we didn't like the idea." But at the same time, Harry thought, "It will never affect me anyway, because I'm going to college." Like others who entered college in the fall of 1966, Harry received the 2-S deferment. Mel Farmer, who joined the army rather than wait for the inevitable draft notice, and who served in Vietnam as a convoy driver, bought the Cold War atmosphere of his high school years: "I remember that missile crisis; it was a scary time. I was glad Kennedy . . . he showed them what was what—you're either going to turn it around or we'll come and get you; that was good." He admits, "Everyone was sort of brainwashed, but concerned about Communism; you know, they kept taking over smaller countries." Mel didn't seek military service: "I figured if I would enlist, maybe I'd have a chance of picking where I want to go, and not getting sent to Vietnam." In September 1966, he went off to Fort Dix for basic and then intensive training, sixteen weeks in all. Like most of his fellow trainees, he got shipped out at Christmastime, to Vietnam.

Matt Blake says, "I would do anything that I had to do not to go; that was my own feeling," despite growing up the son of a World War II veteran. "Not that I wouldn't fight for my country," he adds, but somehow not in this war. Judd Dennis shared this reluctance to risk being "in the bushes over there"; instead, he joined the Coast Guard for four years. He didn't understand why we were fighting in Vietnam: "I knew no one who could define it, and they're still having trouble defining why we were there, and even at that time, there were some against, people going to Canada." Judd knew this secondhand and quickly qualifies, "I didn't want to disgrace my family nor myself by going to Canada." To these graduates, open resistance or avoidance—for example, protest, conscientious objection, flight—were beyond the pale. Yet at the same time, many sought more socially acceptable means to minimize possible Vietnam service—what I call "respectable" draft evasion.

There were exceptions, like Bobby Green or Dave Ford, an upper-middle-class kid who hung out with the rowdies; he received his draft notice while still a high school junior. Dave, influenced by his parents, immediately joined the navy reserve, which allowed him to graduate before starting boot camp. He looked forward to active duty: "I felt real good about being in the service because I was a rah-rah American kid, and I still am; I'm an American and proud of it too." But, he adds, most of his fellow reservists didn't share his enthusiasm. And when given the chance to be "a boatswain's mate on a swift boat in the Mekong Delta with a life span of about four days," Dave elected the safer option of more advanced training. Dan Vitale, also patriotic ("I'm the type of guy who salutes the flag," he tells me), admits that "when I had the choice of going there—in the navy you had to volunteer, unless the whole unit was sent—I turned it down." Thus, even baby boomers with the most flag-waving propensities felt little inclination to choose combat in Vietnam.

To many, the confusion about the war centered on its undeclared, seemingly restrained aspects. Jimmy O'Brien, protected by a heart murmur, flat feet, and a host of other disabilities that made his failure at the physical a foregone conclusion, says, "I could never understand it, totally, why we were there. If we were there, let's go all out; what's the sense of going into a fight if you're going to use one hand? All through history, World War I, World War II, we fought all out and did everything we could to beat the enemy." Such feelings were the rule. Dave Ford believes that "everybody liked Nixon at the time" because he said he would end the war. Nixon supporters like Dave were reenforced while in the service: "I was taught through the military to believe what they wanted me to believe. The people out on the streets don't know what war's about, unless they've actually been there." So concerns about the war rarely led to protests; instead, most invested in the Nixon administration's quest for "peace with honor." And most had a rising intolerance for the protesters.

Regarding Vietnam, the class of 1966 divides along gender lines but also between males going off to college and 2-S deferments and those immediately facing the draft. Social-class background was significant in distinguishing the two paths, but enough exceptions exist in both categories to mandate caution in making any claims of a strict class determinism. In one instance, a college-bound graduate, Tom Rogers, justified privilege rather glibly: "I felt that Vietnam was for the dummies, the losers." Interestingly, Rogers himself was from a lower-income family. Since class lines flattened toward the middle, few of the "dummies, the losers" came from these South Jersey suburban towns; most were at a distance, in blue-collar and poor city neighborhoods and in backwater small towns and farms.

For those going off to college, there were few instances of the kinds of experiences conventionally associated with campus antiwar protest. Sally Vincent Rogers has more memories about the space program than of foreign affairs crises. Although her husband, Tom, pooh-poohs it, Sally speaks proudly of her activist period at Glassboro State College: "There were a big group of us that were very active politically, marching against Vietnam, creating a huge banner," traveling to Trenton for a demonstration. Sally was involved in student government; she recalls working on a huge Christmas card and an "I Love You" banner for GIs in Vietnam. Interestingly, Sally, already married, never spoke about her antiwar views or activities with her conservative parents. "I didn't bring that home; I wasn't an organizer," she admits. "I was more or less a follower." She was delighted when Tom's lottery number was high enough to minimize his chances of being drafted. "He would have gone in; I disagreed with the war, and I wanted it over because I thought it was unfounded, that we had no business being there; I'm sure Tom felt the same way, but you don't have a choice in these matters." Sally and Tom were among those mainstream Americans shifting against the war by the time of the Moratorium in the fall of 1969; they were political moderates, uncomfortable with activism, but, at least regarding Sally, willing to join the more respectable antiwar opposition.

There were a few more antiwar voices, but, like Sally Rogers, most kept at the margins and were often more comfortable with the cultural aspects of campus rebellion. Countercultural experimentation did cut across antiwar feelings, but I haven't found any example of significant involvement in antiwar activism among the graduates of the class of 1966. Most characteristic perhaps are the feelings and experiences of Polly Bain Smythe, who also attended Glassboro State College, preparing to become a teacher. From a fairly protected, religious home, she found college an eye-opener and was attracted to almost all of the dissent and protest she encountered. She says, "In college, I began to challenge everything that I had been taught, politically." She "wanted to be seen as a hippie, absolutely, but didn't have the guts to go out and join the marches." Something in Polly's background, her strict, Methodist upbringing, her self-consciousness, her lack of contact with anybody who had ever rebelled against authority constrained her. Protest was simply out of character. Polly Bain Smythe rejected Nixon's call for a silent-majority answer to campus rebellions, but she found it impossible to break through her inhibitions. Like many on campus, probably the majority, at least away from the elite institutions, she remained silent. She rooted for the protesters, envied them their courage, but held back.

Most graduates who went on to college did not experience even such milder, muted forms of protest and activism. They went to fairly conservative private or public colleges and universities, often in the South. A significant number joined fraternities and sororities; many focused on preparing for their postcollegiate careers. Some, like the Rogerses, married while still in school. Those from lower- to middle-middle income families, worked to pay for college expenses. They had little sympathy for students with the time to protest government policies. And they often knew no one serving in Vietnam. For the more collegiate of this class of 1966, Vietnam—the war itself and the controversy surrounding it—remained distant from and marginal to their lives.

Those serving in Vietnam faced a different reality. By the time Bobby Green arrived in Vietnam in early 1968, "the word's out; guys are coming back and saying, 'Hey, you can't do this, you can't do that,' finding out the war was not the old 'win 'em' thing." On Bobby's first night at Kontum "there was a racial fight which scared the hell out of me." He had been assigned to work on generators but didn't like the work, so he volunteered for the convoys that went back and forth between Kontum and Pleiku in the central highlands, a thirty-five-mile run. It was risky, mostly because of Vietcong sniping, but Bobby adds, "The whole time I was over there nobody got hurt bad, some wounded; I wasn't in the bush too much." Still, his frustration built: "The war was starting to change in my mind; what's going on, you know, we could be winning this? Okay, you hear, they're bombing certain military installations in North Vietnam. I'm not a warmonger, but sometimes total war is the only way you could win a war." However, his anger focused on the brass: "Hamburger Hill happened when I was there. I'm blaming the military officers; it seems like they enjoyed the war. They're in Saigon at night and fly around the battlefield during the day, kind of like what happened in World War I, where they sent those millions of boys into those machine guns—'Send us more bodies.'" Bobby jokes about his ignorance concerning the peace movement: "Soldiers are coming from other military installations; they're going like this to me [he makes a V peace sign]; I thought it meant victory, that's the honest truth." By the time he returned to the States, Bobby Green was "swaying to the protesters' side." Yet he never considered joining antiwar vet groups like the Vietnam Veterans Against the War. He now had long hair, experimented with drugs, and felt rebellious, but he had no thoughts of activism—and neither did any of his friends.

Mel Farmer, who also drove trucks in Vietnam, considers himself lucky to have escaped the infantry. He remembers the suffocating heat and the poverty of the Vietnamese, many of whom, he feels, "didn't care for us." He came to see the war as senseless; he asks, "Weren't we getting near a recession at that time?" But his conclusion that we shouldn't ever have gone there never tempted him to act: "I wouldn't protest against it or run to Canada or nothing like that." In fact, he got mad at the protesters, especially Jane Fonda: "I still hold that against those people. It's America; you can voice your opinion, but it doesn't help the people who's over there fighting. You're against those people." He believes that protesters have the right not to fight, but "at least do your time. You can type; you can do something." Mel adds, "Basically I came back the way I left." When he landed in Philadelphia, he decided to take a limo home. "I didn't have my uniform on, and the guy in the limo said, 'Where were you?' And I said, 'I just came back from Vietnam.' And everyone's asking how it is and all that, and I tell them, 'Atlantic City.' And he says, 'Hey soldier, no charge.'" But, Mel adds, after this pleasant welcome, "nobody really seemed to care. In fact, when I got back, you'd hit a couple of parties; I felt like an outcast." "The ones that didn't go," he suggests, made him feel unwanted. They were antiwar, he continues, but they saw him as a sucker. "'Why did you go?' type thing; I really didn't have a choice, that's why. I just felt let down; nobody really wanted to talk about it then. If you don't talk about it, nobody's going to say anything." So Mel Farmer stored away his experiences and feelings and began to get on with his life.

Not all had easy adjustments; Bobby Green fell into a partying life that verged on the self-destructive. Joey Campion speaks of one marine veteran who went berserk at a local tavern when an army guy bad-mouthed the corps's efforts in the war: "You weren't in Vietnam; you don't know." Military life itself could be difficult; in at least three instances, local baby boomers went AWOL from the service for considerable lengths of time, hiding in shore-area motels from the MPs.

Those who married and started families right out of high school probably had the smoothest transitions to adulthood and were least troubled by the Vietnam War. Their deferments rested on fatherhood. They focused on building careers, saving for a house, and paying the bills. For such high school sweetheart couples, the Sixties, as a decade of rebellion, did not exist except from afar. And they often had no contact with either Vietnam GIs or peaceniks. The war was, at most, a few minutes on the nightly news.

The experiences of those who chose what remains the characteristic South Jersey baby-boom option, the reserves or National Guard, varied the most. Such an option was the preferred and respectable way to resolve the dilemma of both upholding one's patriotic duty and avoiding Vietnam service. It was what Lawrence M. Baskir and William A. Strauss call "one of the routes especially designed for the thinking man" (xvi). Approximately one million draft-eligible baby boomers entered reserve or guard units during the Vietnam War years.

Stan Burke grew up hard-nosed about foreign policy: "I knew that Castro was a son of a bitch, and we should have thrown him out of Cuba; I thought the Bay of Pigs was a good try, but they botched it." While attending a technical college, he avoided any involvement in campus rebellion, little of which was occurring at his institution: "I had no interest in demonstrating against the war or anything else for that matter, really; I was interested in doing what I wanted to do." In fact, he was interested in getting a security clearance to apply for work in intelligence. But he ended up at the phone company, still having to decide how to handle his military service. Stan states emphatically, "I wasn't particularly thrilled with the idea of crawling around in a rice paddy, shooting people—not that I wouldn't have if that's the way it would have worked out." But he made an effort to ensure that that wouldn't be his destiny, letting the navy reserve, where he had contacts, know that he was a ham operator: "He [the recruiter] almost jumped over the desk, grabbed me; I signed the papers, and they jumped me over a six-month waiting list." Stans adds, "So I guess you could say I pulled a 'Dan Quayle.'" (Our interview occurred when the controversy over the selection of George Bush's running mate was at its height.) Stan continues, without prompting, "I did exactly the same thing he did. His parents may or may not have exerted some influence, but the man did serve; it wasn't as if he didn't. This whole thing has been blown out of proportion. It's ridiculous; find me a congressman or find me a senator who hasn't used his pull for some purpose."

Harry Kearns was sitting in his college fraternity, "with pizza and beer and having a grand old time," when the lottery drawing occurred in late 1969. After the first fifty numbers were called, "the phone rang; it was my mother. She said, 'We made it to fifty, we won't have any problems now. My little boy's not going to war.'" And while on the phone, his number was called: "Fifty-two, fifty-three, or fifty-six, I can't remember, and she started crying; she just burst into tears and after a few minutes we settled her down and I said, 'Mom, I'll take care of it.'" Harry was looking forward to student teaching, a career, graduate school; in April he received his draft notice. He went home to go for his physical, but "in the meantime, I didn't know this, my father—it's ironic that we're talking about this now, because this is what's going on through [the] Quayle [controversy]—my father made a few phone calls and talked to friends of his in the National Guard." Harry indicated to the guard that his education could meet their need for instructors. He is highly agitated as he tells this story: "Half of us were going to Vietnam; half of us were being sent back to our units. It really upsets me to hear them talking about the National Guard the way it was, because we could have been called at any time."

In basic training, Harry felt like "the National Guard were treated like dirt, until they realized that we were all college graduates, that we all had something to offer and that they might as well use our talents, while we were there, to train these other people, make it a little easier for them, who probably were going to go to Vietnam." Harry's platoon included a Harvard Law School graduate, an engineer, and two other teachers; they became the squad leaders: "They used us in the training roles, as models, because most of the other boys were black or poor southern boys who had enlisted, and their whole life was to enlist in the army." Harry's training was rigorous, but it left him with mixed emotions about Vietnam: "I didn't think we should have been there. I personally didn't want to go there. I didn't want to go to war for the sake of going to war; it wouldn't have mattered if it was Vietnam or Korea, Europe, or anywhere. As a young person, twenty, twenty-one years old, I didn't really understand like I do today what was going on in Vietnam. It would seem to me at the time that it was a senseless war, that we were sending people over there to be killed for absolutely no reason whatsoever." But Harry Kearns has changed his mind over the years: "I now see a reason why we had to be there," although, he qualifies, "I'm still not sure I agree with it. I can now see why we have to do what we have been doing in Nicaragua; I can see why we have to be careful in Panama. I can see the same types of things happening, and I can think back—I was probably thinking very selfish back in the Sixties and I was thinking of 'I' instead of the country." Harry now follows current events religiously in the daily newspaper. He isn't convinced that the United States has learned any lessons from the Vietnam War. He doesn't watch any of the commercially popular Vietnam War movies: "Subconsciously I think I avoided them; consciously I just haven't gone out of my way to . . . they're not types of things I want to remember. I see [how] it was [and think] 'Jeez, I could have been there.' That bothers me still to a point."

Whatever is bothering Harry Kearns, he admires Dan Quayle because "he reminds me of myself and he's got to stand up and fight for something he really shouldn't have to stand up and fight for, as far as I'm concerned. It just kind of ticks me off, to see a guy go through what he's going through." Harry concludes, "He didn't do anything illegal. Bush said, 'He didn't burn an American flag; he didn't flee to Canada.' That's true." Harry Kearns has been an active member of the American Legion for twenty years.

Others voice mixed feelings about the choices they made. Judd Dennis's wife, Susan, recalls, "We ate dinner to the death marches; we ate dinner to the death toll in Vietnam, what was going on, who, how many of our boys were killed, the blood bath." She interjects, "I had brothers in Vietnam." Judd admits, "Sometimes I feel a little guilty because I was able to go into the Coast Guard and get out of it and knowing that 90 percent of those guys didn't really want to be there." Then he adds, expressing what I think is the predominant sentiment, "But they were like me—if you were drafted, you went, and if I had been drafted, I would have went. I wouldn't have wanted to." Susan, one of whose brothers suffers from problems caused by Agent Orange, bitterly concludes, "What did Vietnam teach me? It taught me that the government doesn't tell you the truth."

Susan Dennis's responses, while not unique, are more decisive than those of most graduates. A lot of queasiness and confusion still exists about the war and about those who fought it.
Many of these white middle-class baby boomers could use
connections to beat the draft, but essentially their middle-class
environment created the possibilities behind their own backs.
Life in mainstream Middle America comes with built-in privileges; such benefits acquired through the use of family and
community networks are part of the informal system that gives
an edge to their children. And they are available even to many
of those from the least-privileged working-class families who
derive advantage from their whiteness and from their community membership. The invisibility of social-class, gender, and
racial advantages, particularly in a nonelite environment like
these South Jersey suburban towns, is critical to any effort to
understand Middle American life and culture. Middle-class
baby boomers could feel unease, but rarely chose to act in ways
that put them at risk.

And the suburban cocoon is often sustained by an abysmal
ignorance of history. The high school rarely inspired or encouraged curiosity or knowledge about the world. In the
years since 1966, few graduates have paid much attention to
history, politics, or international affairs. Matt Blake credits
Gerald Ford with pulling us out of Vietnam and would still
vote for Nixon, "even though he was the one who committed" troops to Vietnam. "Wasn't it Nixon?" he asks, and then
concludes, "But I don't hold him responsible for it; I blame
whoever was in office to begin with, which was Johnson?"
Aggie Jones Rizzuto, whose husband served in the navy, feels
the war as remote, in part because no one seems willing to
talk about it: "Nobody got killed, and to my knowledge I
haven't met anybody who didn't come home and pick up

their life; you know, they show you the things where they have hallucinations, they can't get themselves back together. Fortunately, I don't know anybody that that happened to."

Some 1966 graduates do watch the movies and televison shows about Vietnam that, for awhile flooded the airwaves. George Evanson, a 4-F, after watching the acclaimed HBO documentary "Dear America," felt embarrassed about how little he knew: "I was asking my wife, 'Did you ever know anybody. . .what did you think about this?' And she said, 'It never bothered me.' And I said, 'Did you know anybody that died?' And she said, 'No.' And I said, 'Neither did I.' I don't know anybody. It was very removed; the war always continued to be of some distance. I never really knew what was going on except that we were fighting for a cause." George had a colleague who had served in Vietnam: "He would tell stories about stuff he used to do, and I used to call him a liar and say, 'You're crazy.' He would say, 'We used to get them up in a helicopter and throw them out of the helicopter.' [I said,] 'We wouldn't do that stuff!' And he said, 'We're as bad as everybody else,' and he was really . . . I said, 'John, why are you telling me this?' He said, 'It's the truth, we used to go up, asking questions, and if the first one wouldn't answer, we'd push him out of the helicopter.' I said, 'Nah' . . . I was absolutely shocked." George Evanson, who still avoids foreign affairs news, represents a significant segment of silent-majority baby boomers. Because of his circumstances—for example, his lack of combat experience, his lack of significant contact with Vietnam veterans, his avoidance of mass media presentations touching on the war's pain, his lack of any contact with antiwar activists—George is able to sidestep coming to grips with the realities of Vietnam and is shocked when occasionally forced to face such realities.

Mac Schmidt, whose old football injuries would have kept him out even if he hadn't married and started a family right out of high school, stopped watching the news on television because, he says, "I'm a very contented person, happy-go-lucky-type guy; I'd have a nice day at work, come home, and watch this crap on the news, and it would screw me up—I depressed myself. So why expose [myself] to that?" The war made him angry, but he adds, "I really didn't have real strong political beliefs, ties, feelings; we didn't get involved, still don't." He ignored the Hollywood films until renting the *Platoon* video. He couldn't finish it: "It got too heavy. This is horrible. These poor guys are sloshing through the mud; people are being cut up. And when I finally turned it off, it was when they went into the village, and one of the soldiers beat a young boy to death with the butt of his rifle. I could sense the frustration of not being able to identify who the enemy was, but I can't believe we were there to abuse those people like that. You have this wonderful little village, this idyllic night, and we're going over and rape women and beat them to death and kill their pigs—I'm sure a pig was worth quite a bit." He was deeply shocked and surprised by such atrocities: "Yeah, I'd avoided the whole thing. I'd just as soon not know, really; it's too heavy. Same attitude as I had in '68—why screw up my life?"

For these suburban baby boomers the antiwar activism that often is portrayed as characteristic of college students, even as faddish, was at best marginal and most typically nonexistent. To actively oppose the Vietnam War seemed alien, odd, out of character. Most 1966 graduates find it almost unimaginable to protest openly, demonstrate, or engage in more conventionally defined electoral political activity regarding U.S. foreign policy. More than 70 percent voted for

Nixon in their 1972 initiation into electoral politics. Activism runs against the grain of their upbringing. These behaviors are not reducible to selfishness or narcissism, as suggested by some cultural critics. For the most part, these people care about others; however, their caring tends to stop at the borders of the family, the neighborhood, and the local community. They have built walls to protect themselves from aspects of modernity they mistrust and fear. Ultimately, their justification rests on their ignorance. If they have derived lessons from Vietnam, these have been muted. They don't rally around the flag as easily as their World War II parents did; at least they didn't until the Persian Gulf War. Somalia and Bosnia remain remote and impossible to fathom. They aren't as willing to risk American lives; they have more skepticism about the rhetoric of their government. At the same time, they tend to vote for conservative, defense-oriented Republicans who until the 1990s sought to overcome what Ronald Reagan called the Vietnam syndrome. Some don't vote or have few expectations when they do. So long as such essentially decent but parochial people remain a silent majority, the lessons of Vietnam will be limited to the view that U.S. military interventions will be supported or, at the least, tolerated as long as the risk to American lives remains minimal. It's no wonder that Bill Clinton's draft history generates such emotional responses. Until our reconstruction of the history of the war includes a serious consideration of those, like these Middle American suburban baby boomers, whose responses were so characteristically ambivalent, who are made nervous by the veterans who brought the war home, who project some of their guilt and shame onto those who openly protested, who are determined not to learn from the past, we will have less than a complete accounting.

5

Identity Politics: Snatching Defeat from the Jaws of Victory

In a provocative *New Yorker* essay, Gregg Easterbrook, after bemoaning the tendency for environmentalism "to be dominated by images of futility, crisis, and decline," asks, "Why not trumpet the astonishing, and continuing, record of success in environmental protection?" Easterbrook persuasively makes the case that the past twenty-five years have seen extraordinary accomplishments, such as cleaner water and air, decreases in smog, a decline in toxic hazards, actual reforestation, and species protection.

As Easterbrook cautions, such impressive progress is not to be taken as a signal to back off from a rigorous attending to risks, especially in the developing Third World and around the issue of the dismantling of nuclear arsenals. The recent Republican assault on environmental protection, indeed, rests on the ideological conviction that governmental interventions are inherently counterproductive to liberty, security, and efficiency. Easterbrook convincingly demonstrates the very opposite. And all survey research suggests that the American people remain strongly committed to environmental protection, seeing it as a necessary example of governmental activism.

What Easterbrook is getting at is the tendency of some environmentalists to anticipate doomsday, to focus on failures in ways that dovetail with the conservative ideological assaults on the role of government in all areas except those related to the military and law enforcement. I would take things one step further, albeit carefully: Some on the fringes of the environmental movement not only anticipate but desire catastrophic outcomes in their ideological aversion to modern, industrial culture. Like their allies in the identity politics movements—African Americans, women, gays, and lesbians—some radical ecologists find accomplishment within the established polity positively counterintuitive.

I don't join Easterbrook in calling for all of us to become "environmental optimists"; my preference is to hold to Antonio Gramsci's stance of "pessimism of the intellect; optimism of the will." There's certainly enough at risk in a world suffering from genocidal civil strife, high-tech terrorism, a global AIDS epidemic, and deepening poverty in Africa and Latin America.

However, I do wish to raise a series of questions about what we might call half-full and half-empty narratives concerning the natural world, gender politics, and race relations. Too often I hear, especially from those who proclaim solidarity with the legacy of Sixties movements, of the turn to the right since that decade, of the rise of Reaganism, of the assault on civil and women's rights, of the backlash against all liberatory movements. In regards to racial matters, it is certainly true—

and needs to be forcefully emphasized—that for many African Americans life is worse by a whole series of measures, including family dysfunction, incarceration, crack-cocaine epidemics, unemployment, declining welfare benefits. At the same time, there seems to be a need among those left of center to deny the very real and astounding progress that has been made. Part of this, as Easterbrook notes, rests on the fear that celebrating successes will play into the hands of those wishing to call a halt to government programs—the present controversies over affirmative action are a case in point. Have we come far enough? Is it needed any longer?

I prefer to argue that this aversion to recognizing the contradictory accomplishments of the 1960s plays into the hands of those on the Right who blame all contemporary social ills on that tumultuous decade. Implicit in this aversion, I believe, is a radical resistance to recognizing the tenuous but very real capacity of the liberal welfare state to expand human and civil rights as it walks its tightrope between capitalist profit-maximization and a democratic commitment to social justice.

Civil Rights, Black Power, and the Poverty Wars

The year was 1965. It was an uplifting lecture. James Silver, a history professor from the University of Mississippi and the author of *Mississippi: The Closed Society,* spoke of how heartening it was to see the beginnings of the breakdown of Jim Crow and lynch law. He was eloquent and modest. He had challenged southern taboos, been driven out of the state, and was there to tell us, a Rutgers University audience mainly of white students, that, for the first time in his life, he felt hopeful about the South's future.

When he finished, to a standing ovation, he fielded questions from a mostly worshipful audience. Then a voice came from the back of the large lecture hall: "I'm from Jersey City, and I already can vote—don't make no difference—and sit anywhere I want, but I live with bad housing, schools, no jobs. Is all that you're saying is that the South will be like Jersey City?" Silver responded thoughtfully, trying to hold together his hopefulness with a recognition that desegregation was a necessary but insufficient reform. The audience felt uncomfortable. It wanted, if for just that moment, to feel good about the country and its ability to remedy historical injustices; it resented the young black man's troubling comments.

Two events of 1965 provide the beginnings of a framework for understanding the legacy of the racial politics of the 1960s: the Watts riot and the controversies surrounding Daniel Patrick Moynihan's study of the crisis within the black family.

The riot in Watts was not the first of the decade; 1964 saw violence erupt in New York, Philadelphia, and Rochester. But the Watts riot was larger, more destructive, less containable, and therefore more powerful in its impact. The cynicism of that young black man from Jersey City was writ large as small incidents set off what were essentially consumer riots, dominated by the looting of local stores, initially by youth, but soon by a surprising cross-section of the ghetto population. At the time of the Newark riot, a local resident described it to me as "a festival" of theft, of appropriating what had been denied because of historical injustices, that is, racism.

The Watts riot occurred soon after the release of Moynihan's report, which, consistent with prevailing liberal and civil rights perspectives, worried about the consequences of a culture of poverty and the increasingly dysfunctional families it seemed to be generating. Moynihan's historical analysis proved to be inadequate (female-headed households were not a legacy of slavery and the Jim Crow era), but his overview and his concern—that poverty was declining, dependency on AFDC (Aid to Families with Dependent Children) was rising, and black families were eroding—seemed accurate and persuasive to many of those with histories of a commitment to civil rights. After the Watts riot, most black leaders and many white liberals repudiated Moynihan as "blaming the victim," as shifting attention from poverty, unemployment, and racism toward a psychopathology of the oppressed.

The elimination of de facto segregation and the movement of the United States toward formal equality of opportunity, including voting rights were established in law by 1965 with the passage of the Civil Rights Act and the Voting Rights Act. The interesting question is why, at precisely the moment when fundamental historical change was occurring, when the nation seemed to finally be taking up the mantle of equal rights, did the African American community (at least its most vocal leaders and activists) view seeming allies like Moynihan as the enemy? Why did so many experience despair and rage and turn toward a more nationalist, separatist, and radical politics? The Jersey City man's comments offer a necessary but not sufficient explanation.

At the Democratic Party's 1964 convention in Atlantic City, another aspect of this fundamental change occurred. The Mississippi Freedom Democratic Party (MFDP) felt betrayed by the national Democrats, especially by such old friends as Joe Rauh and Hubert Humphrey. How could liberals accept an immoral compromise that allowed the segregationist state party to maintain their seats when the MFDP's cause was so just, so compelling? How could the MFDP accept two token seats at large, preselected by the party leadership, when they were carrying with them the hopes and dreams of the black people of the Mississippi Delta?

Yet by 1968 the Democratic Party had fulfilled its promise; it had mandated integrated state delegations. When one reads the literature of this period, 1964–1967, one is struck with a kind of cognitive dissonance. How could people be so angry and down when so many things seemed so hopeful and up?

A dozen or so years later, William Julius Wilson published *The Declining Significance of Race.* Many of my colleagues, white and black, placed Wilson's study within the category of "neoconservative," linking Wilson with thinkers such as Glenn Loury, Walter Williams, and Thomas Sowell. When I finally got around to reading it, I was astounded to discover that Wilson was a European-style social democrat, a believer in state interventions within a capitalist economy, a sociologist interested in the ways in which the civil rights revolution, in opening educational and therefore career opportunities for upwardly mobile blacks, had created a new situation in which the social-class variations between African Americans had become salient. Wilson was concerned with the implications of this gap and clearly wished to have more attention focused on those left behind, like the fellow from Jersey City. Why were so many black and white radicals and liberals determined to place Wilson in the enemy camp?

Perhaps part of the answer can be gleaned from Wilson's more recent study *The Truly Disadvantaged,* in which he argues that liberals "have been reluctant to discuss openly or, in some instances, even to acknowledge the sharp increase in social pathologies in ghetto communities" (16). Indeed, Wilson suggested that the "virulent attacks against Moynihan" (15) back in the middle and late 1960s intimidated scholars from studying the most important social phenomena of a black underclass.

When one reviews the literature of the civil rights movement, one is impressed with the rising rage and alienation of young African American activists, particularly those associated with SNCC. What drove their depair and, importantly, their hopes for a revolutionary politics, especially at the time of the passage of the Civil Rights Act and the Voting Rights Act? It is here that the civil rights movement intertwines with the 1960s—with the critique of the welfare state and with the eruption of the war in Vietnam.

The developing New Left, powerfully influenced by black activists, increasingly found itself moving beyond the liberal-laborite alliance strategy still central to the Port Huron Statement. But by 1963–1964 and certainly by 1965, the white student New Left was moving toward a populist, anticapitalist sensibility—it wasn't yet a theory—that stressed alienation over exploitation and race over class, and that increasingly identified with Third World revolutionaries such as Fidel Castro, Mao Zedong, and, shortly, Ho Chi Minh and the VC. The black power movement, which only became visible to most Americans during the 1966 James Meredith March, was already on the rise by Mississippi Freedom Summer, which heightened nationalist and separatist resentments. Malcolm X was already drawing more interest than Dr. King; and Third World figures, from Kwame Nkrumah and Patrice Lumumba to Che Guevara, were the objects of admiration and imitation.

The issue here is Third Worldism, that is, the romance white and black activists had with the notion, most associated with Lin Baio and the Great Chinese Proletarian Cultural Revolution, that the class struggle was now global, with the countrysides of Asia, Africa, and Latin America in rebellion against the imperial cities of Europe and America. One can already hear the late 1960s ultraromanticism in Tom Hayden's descriptions of southern black sharecroppers as less alienated, less corrupted by bourgeois values and behaviors. It is this romance with the poor as precapitalist, non-Western, nonwhite that then fused with Third World liberation metaphors during the mid-1960s, especially as the Vietnam War became the embodiment of this populist and utopian narrative.

Is it any wonder that the 1964 Democratic National Convention in Atlantic City produced such a deeply painful rift between party liberals and movement activists? The very notion of "the Movement," a community resting on authenticity, on the experimental, experiential life, on commitment, ran flush up against what historians refer to as the Johnson treatment—arm-twisting, seducing, flattering, intimidating, full-court pressure to stand with the party's new and very powerful candidate, to maintain institutional loyalty, to play the game. To SNCC and its allies the game was emblematic of the corruption of the System. At certain levels of their feelings and emerging ideology, Movement activists did not want a piece of Johnson's Great Society, his ambitious, overreaching effort to carry the New Deal of his idol, FDR, to completion. Tom Hayden and Bob Moses wanted "the beloved community," which itself was rapidly unraveling, not an American welfare state; they wanted participatory democracy, not a brokered bourgeois democracy. They wanted . . . well, they weren't always sure what they wanted and were moving further apart even in defining its direction, but they knew what they *didn't* want, and that was what LBJ and Humphrey and Walter Mondale and Walter Reuther and Allard Lowenstein were offering—a piece of the action.

So the tragedy of Atlantic City was that the choices of both parties reenforced the stereotypes each had of the other. Johnson's forces would write off the MFDP as unserious and utopian; Movement types would be reenforced in their belief that liberals were inherently corrupt and unworthy of respect.

Among contemporary African American intellectuals, the rise of black power remains a source of much contention. The best-case argument is that even with the first openings of opportunity coming with the end of Jim Crow and the gestures of the Great Society and its War on Poverty, there remained the problematic of DuBois's double consciousness: American and African. Even well-intentioned whites such as the historian Kenneth Stampp had suggested that blacks were only white faces with black masks. The distinctive estrangement blacks experienced within their American historical experience did not allow for the kinds of assimiliation available to European immigrants. The harsh, hateful welcome Martin Luther King, Jr., received during his Chicago open-housing campaigns gave some measure of how pervasive was the racial divide. The end of legal segregation hardly resolved an institutionalized, entrenched legacy of discrimination and bigotry. Given such conditions, those championing black power and its essential voice, Malcolm X, have a strong case in arguing that, as Stokely Carmichael stated, individuals assimilate, groups integrate. Black Americans needed to become a group, develop an identity that valued their history, their culture, their language, their accomplishments, their very identities. Otherwise, the traditional ladder of upward mobility was skewed toward cultural, racial self-contempt and suicide. How could one *become* an American without betraying a particularly stigmatized racial identity? Others *chose* the United States; blacks—and native Americans—had the United States imposed on them. One need not buy the full implications of Leroi Jones's (Amiri Baraka) *The Dutchman* with its white she-serpent seducing, stripping, and then murdering the Bigger Thomas within every buttoned-down middle-class black to acknowledge that desegregation was easier to achieve than integration and that the melting-pot metaphor offered little comfort and loads of terror for African Americans.

Revolutionary movements lose their integrity when they begin to cover unpleasant facts with rhetorical rationalizations. The Bolsheviks, for example, could make at least a cogent case for a Communist Party dictatorship as the only alternative to a right-wing, military one. But in stretching beyond any semblance of social reality the already problematic concept of a dictatorship of the proletariat, that is, to insist that the workers were still in charge—after Kronstadt—was to guarantee a corruption of all ideals. The decline of Communism began at that moment. In the case of black power and various forms of nationalism and separatism, an analogous process occurred.

Perhaps the first issue to address is the inappropriateness of a revolutionary model of any type to frame racial politics, from Black Panther communism to Nation of Islam separatism. When African Americans wear sweatshirts quoting Malcolm X, "By any means necessary," what do they mean to communicate? Is it a racial pride that includes the right to self-defense against racist attack, or is it a call to arms? How much is it a rhetorical gesture, a "mau-mauing" of frightened whites?

By the late 1960s such a rhetorical style had become common in African American activism. (Let me make very clear that the largest number of black political actors focused attention on more mundane and pragmatic efforts to build their communities, improve their schools, and provide support for those most in need. But such work, precisely because it assumed the permanence of the prevailing social order and sought incremental improvements, was never able to effectively challenge the rhetorical extravagances of the militants.) Malcolm X set the tone. The sanctification of Malcolm over the past several decades obscures the destructive dimensions of his legacy. It's not only Malcolm's sexism or his anti-Semitism—these can in part be explained by the transformations he was going through at the time of his death. It's his dogmatic, rhetorical style, his sticking it to whitey; precisely those qualities of racial assertiveness and pride, the bombast and excess, distinguish Malcolm from his integrationist and liberal rivals.

Thus, in attacking Moynihan it wasn't sufficient to view him as a misguided ally; he had to be excoriated as a racist, an enemy—and the issues he raised were therefore grounds for excommunication from the Movement, white and black. As was true with much of Sixties activism, black power politics absolutized all issues. As Eldridge Cleaver asserted, "You're either part of the problem or part of the solution."

This was an assault on all forms of liberalism, including democratic socialism—a good-bye to all that moderation, to maybes and perhapses, to irony and paradox and ambiguity. Indeed, with the rising violence of both Indochina and the ghetto riots driving one's sense of urgency, it was virtually impossible not to obsess on one's commitment, one's willingness to risk, even to die for social justice. And it was a utopian moment, with a variety of visions contesting and often converging and merging: a Third World vision of peasant warriors; Che Guevara's vision of "the new socialist man," selfless, communal, renaissance; countercultural visions of sexual liberation, psychedelic mind-fucks, and a Woodstock Nation dancing in the streets and strawberry fields; Charles

Reich's Con III; SDS notions of a revolutionary youth movement aligned with racial minorities, white working-class youth, and the countryside Viet Cong; visions of people of color struggling against those unwilling to give up their white-skin privileges; visions of sisterhood; visions of all against Amerikkka, in the belly of the beast; visions of there being "no country and no religion too"; visions of urban guerrilla warfare, inspired by Frantz Fanon and Regis Debray and the Living Theatre and Jean-Paul Sartre and Allen Ginsberg and Timothy Leary and Mao and Fidel and Ho and *The Battle of Algiers* and *Bonnie and Clyde* and Bob Dylan and Carlos Casteneda and Wilhelm Reich and Herbert Marcuse.

The Black Panthers perhaps most embodied these contradictory, utopian, and essentially theatrical currents. The Panthers were our first post-civil rights urban movement; Huey Newton and Bobby Seale reacted to de facto segregation and poverty and, in particular, to police brutalities. They directed breakfast programs and seemed able to reach out to tough street kids in ways previously achieved only by the Nation of Islam. They were black nationalists but not antiwhite; they were Marxist-Leninists, black communists seeking allies in the New Left movements. And they faced police and domestic intelligence repression of the most severe kind.

What is the legacy of the Black Panthers? Filmmaker Mario Van Peebles and other African American voices, plus many of those still enamored of the revolutionary possibilities of the Sixties, highlight Panther courage and integrity and claim that their demise was a consequence of the threat they posed to the system. In this version, the Black Panthers had to be crushed by a government conspiracy—Hoover, Nixon, CIA. We know enough about such conspiracies, about COINTELPRO, for example, to pay attention to the various extralegalities employed to disrupt, demoralize, divide, and even murder Black Panthers. However, we also know enough about the criminality of the Panthers themselves not to succumb to romanticization.

The Panthers, according to Hugh Pearson, were a street gang, as well as a political movement, from the very beginning. And Huey Newton was a sociopathic, dangerous young man before lionization turned him toward his worst moments of substance abuse. After one reads Pearson and Elaine Brown, it is difficult not to be glad that the Black Panthers failed to achieve political success. They engaged in the drug trade, extortion, the torture of members accused of disloyalty, and a number of murders, none of which can by any measure be excused as self-defense.

Peter Collier and David Horowitz, whose turn to the right fills me with nothing but contempt and nausea, provide a chilling account of how the movement avoided coming to grips with the Panther murder of a bookkeeper suspected of unwittingly coming across evidence of their criminal profits. I can recall in researching my first book, *Philadelphia Communists,* how impressed I was with the painful admission of some of my respondents that if actually in power, instead of being cadre within the always small American Communist Party, CPUSA, they might have engaged in Stalinist executions. They understood how their dogmatic righteousness seduced them into a willingness to declare someone a nonperson and then to coolly, with a clear conscience, imagine eliminating them. The Black Panther leadership, certainly personified by the charismatic Newton, came to such behaviors very early, and all too often without the ideological rationalizations. Of course, one can see similarly murderous desires if not actions in the extremities of the New Left among the Weathermen.

I can recall how in the late 1960s some of us would engage in the game of a top-ten execution list "after the revolution." I did so easily. I called myself a democratic socialist, never a Marxist-Leninist, abhored the turn in the New Left toward dogmatism and ultraradicalism, never saw the Panthers as the vanguard—but I was sufficiently in the midst of the movement to play at postrevolutionary executions.

If one wished to make the best case against the capacity of the United States to become a racially fair society, one could do no better than to read Derrick Bell's *Faces at the Bottom of the Well*, Andrew Hacker's *Two Nations,* and Douglas S. Massey and Nancy A. Denton's *American Apartheid.* Bell presents the most despondent narrative, broad in its testimony, eloquent and stark, simply adding up the history of racism as a permanence. Bell goes beyond a half-empty to a *totally* empty cup:

> Black people will never gain full equality in this country. Even those herculean efforts we hail as successful will produce no more than temporary "peaks of progress," short-lived victories that slide into irrelevance as racial patterns adapt in ways which maintain white dominance. This is a hard-to-accept fact that all history verifies. We must acknowledge it, not as a sign of submission, but as an act of ultimate defiance. (12)

Bell's bleak stoicism leads him to assume that reform-minded efforts "may indeed, despite our best efforts, be of more help to the system we despise than to the victims of that system we are trying to help"(198).

Hacker and Massey and Denton provide the empirical support for such pessimism about racial justice. Massey and Denton demonstrate the extraordinary tenacity, indeed the expansion, of residential segregation and the ways in which this isolation contributes to the making of a racial underclass. They

are most convincing in the distinctions they draw between residential patterns of other minorities, especially Hispanics with
minimal or no African origins, and African Americans. The
former integrate with upward mobility; the latter do not.

Hacker concludes, based on an enormous amount of census data, that the racial divide "is pervasive and penetrating,"
and that "it surpasses all others—even gender—in intensity
and subordination" (3). He offers no solutions and little comfort to those looking for silver linings; he asks white Americans, with no expectation of a productive response, "Is it
right to impose on members of an entire race a lesser start in
life, and then to expect from them a degree of resolution that
has never been demanded from your own race?" (219).

Indeed, there are reasons for such a seemingly hard-
headed pessimism. Racism remains pervasive. Most whites
have no idea of what it's like to be black—looked at with suspicion in stores, unable to get a cab, locked out of suburban
housing markets, up against euphemistic job market categories like "All-American" that are codes for "No blacks need
apply." Such experiences have launched a virtual industry
about the rage of the black middle class.

But such rage finally rests on the remarkable success story
of upwardly mobile African Americans. Infinitely more troubling is the measurable erosion of ghetto life; the deepening
of poverty and unemployment; the collapse of family; the
pathologies of dependency, crime, and drugs; and a syndrome
of self-destructive behaviors associated with the underclass.

This latter set of conditions rests on the tragic confluence,
on the one hand, of what Nicholas Lemann calls "the great
black migration," the process by which African Americans
moved out of the rural South, pulled by opportunity, stimulated by two world wars, and pushed by the mechanization

of cotton agriculture, with, on the other hand, deindustrialization. African Americans came north and to southern and western cities precisely as smokestack industries were declining; therefore, the possibilities of making a living wage, the expectation that they could support a family, began to erode for many black men. This was the setting for the controversies over the Moynihan Report, for the welfare rights battles of the National Welfare Rights Organization for a guaranteed national income, for the ways in which zero-sum policies like affirmative action and busing made it virtually impossible to hold together the multiracial alliance the Democrats needed to sustain a pro-growth, antipoverty politics.

Several African American intellectuals such as Stanley Crouch argue that the success of a black power strategy in the middle to late 1960s was disastrous for African Americans insofar as it encouraged a rhetorical extravagance that favored venting over the necessary work of reconstructing black community life, which was being ravaged by deindustrialization and its disastrous cultural consequences.

As Crouch ferociously asserts, the Third World fantasies of black power played into the romanticism of the cultural Left, enamored of anything and everything that it was *not*— not white, not American, not middle class. This romance, anticipated by Norman Mailer in "The White Negro," identified with the criminal, the insane, the outsider, the non-Westerner, the child—all those not suffocating from bourgeois normality, suburban boredom, philistine materialism. This white bohemian and radical romance with a stereotypical black vitality or "soul" goes back to Carl Van Vechten and 1920s cultural rebels and carries us to today's fascination of white suburban kids with gangsta rap. Tom Wolfe would be one of the first conservative writers to satirize this Sixties slumming in his essays on the Leonard Bernstein fund-raiser for the Black Panthers and on what he called "mau-mauing," the intimidation of guilty white liberals by manipulative black militants. Later he would build an entire novel, *Bonfire of the Vanities,* around the absurd and indeed tragic aspects of this racial tangle.

But one must temper one's admiration for Wolfe's narrative skill with a sober criticism of his seeming obliviousness to the social realities of race and class. In assessing the legacy of the 1960s struggles for equal rights, it's important to take seriously the evidence driving the interpretations of Derrick Bell and others who have given up any hope for a truly nonracist society. The problem is the contradictory evidence that too often brings forth contradictory polarities—the one, à la Bell, viewing U.S. racism as either constant or worsening; the other, claiming that we have already accomplished a race-neutral society. In fact, as in many other instances relating to the influences of the Sixties, we have been going forward, going backward, and standing still in our racial politics over the past quarter of a century.

I believe we will be best served by recognizing the contradictory evidence:

1. Antiblack racism persists and in some important areas has worsened. From the worsening condition of the black underclass to the conservative coded use of race as an electoral trump card (e.g., Willie Horton, affirmative action), we see this bedrock of bigotry.

2. Antiblack racism has been declining; there has been significant, measurable progress in the movement toward Dr. King's notion of treating individuals in terms of their character rather than their skin color. Many white Americans, *including* many who are conservative and vote Republican, have come to adopt more racially tolerant attitudes and behaviors.

3. African American antiwhite racism, a xenophobic hostility to nonblacks (including nonwhites, e.g., Asians, Hispanics), encouraged by some demagogic black intellectuals and activists such as the Nation of Islam, has been increasing.

This contradictory set of realities helps one make sense of what seem so often to be confusing signals and inappropriate responses. Paul M. Sniderman and Thomas Piazza in *The Scar of Race* provide useful explorations into how race and racism intertwine with politics and public policy. They make a persuasive case against the notion that "the primary factor driving contemporary arguments over the politics of race is white racism" (5). For example, they indicate that commitments to conservative policy agendas cannot be reduced to racial prejudice, indeed, that what most correlates with racism is not opposition to welfare or affirmative action but other forms of ethnic prejudice such as anti-Semitism as well as authoritarian personality traits.

Sniderman and Piazza suggest that most white Americans do not think about race very much at all and that when they do their views are remarkably malleable. The most significant case in point is affirmative action. Whereas many whites support efforts to insure that blacks are treated equally, affirmative-action policies are perceived as violating core values like fairness, individuality. Most disturbing are the results of the "mere mention" experiment, which suggests that "merely asking whites to respond to the issue of affirmative action increases significantly the likelihood that they will perceive blacks as irresponsible and lazy" (103).

We presently face a morally confusing challenge. Indeed, there is no question but that conservative leaders are challenging affirmative action as a racial-wedge issue. But for nonconservatives, both ethical and pragmatic concerns remain.

Despite denials, there is a zero-sum quality to the logic of affirmative action, especially as it often tends toward numerical rigidities, that is, quotas. And despite the accurate of claims that preferential treatment toward children of alumni exists in the case of college admissions and is rarely protested by whites, a more formalized, codified, government-sponsored procedure of group-based opportunities remains troubling. That wrongs are committed to privilege alumni children hardly strengthens the case for a different set of wrongs.

At the pragmatic level, we must deal with the ways in which, however well-intentioned in 1965, affirmative action tends to divide groups and play into reactionary hands. At the very least, we need to focus more on the kinds of issues that unite rather than divide potential elements in a progressive coalition. William Julius Wilson is correct to call for more race-neutral social policies, such as minimum-wage increases, guaranteed health care, the earned-income tax credit, and more public investment in various forms of schooling.

The legacy of the 1960s regarding race can be captured by the changes in our predispositions. Up to 1965 or thereabouts, when a black person charged a white person with racism, nonracist whites were predisposed to assume the validity of the allegation. What's changed is, first of all, there are many more nonracist whites. That's great and a too often denied example of progress. Second and more problematical is that many of those nonracist whites are no longer ready to assume the validity of a charge of racism; they are more likely to feel confusion, frustration, even anger at what they perceive to be the moral ambiguity of the situation.

Such moral ambiguity began with the Sixties riots and was deepened by the zero-sum policy issues (e.g., busing and affirmative action), exacerbated by rising black crime rates and associated ghetto-specific behaviors, and battered by the racist demagogy of Louis Farrakhan, Leonard Jeffries, and events such as the Tawana Brawley affair. Instead of right or wrong, events seem to have become white or black, matters of ethnic loyalty rather than affairs of conscience. In such instances, the liberal desire in good faith to respect and respond to African American grievances trips over African American identity politics.

So when a black youth is shot by a white cop, one's inclination is to share the suspicion voiced by the black community that racism played a role in the decision to fire. But the realities of contemporary racial politics make that posture impossible. One holds back, too scarred by experience to wish to be played the fool. Or one remains wary of police misbehaviors and of the tendency of police to cover up for their fellow officers' violations of the law, and yet one feels some solidarity, some empathy for the life-risking realities city police face in an increasingly lawless, violent, and gun-crazed environment.

Indeed, one gain we can chart coming out of the 1960s and civil rights advances is that we have proceeded well past the point of doing what should always have been the case—beginning with the assumption that every group has its glorious history and its moments of shame, its impressive heroes and its cowards and knaves. Being oppressed, being a victim doesn't protect one from such corruptions. Conservatives have too often demagogically highlighted those cowards and knaves, among them Willy Horton and Marion Barry, sterotyped those corruptions. But of course they exist.

The obsession with race tends to obscure the social-class dimensions of the 1960s legacy. The most salient point is that conservatives have succeeded in dominating the story of federal efforts to reduce economic inequities. Most Americans believe that we tried to eliminate poverty and we failed; more-over, we made things worse. This perspective, whose most influential voice has been Charles Murray's, has become a cornerstone of the conservative assault on all public policies that don't address crime, defense, or right-wing morality.

Of course, some of the conservative criticisms are true. The War on Poverty had its share of boondoggles, corruption, and waste; more significantly, many of its programs made little or no headway in remedying poverty. The most important players in this drama have been the neoconservatives, scholars like Nathan Glazer, Daniel Patrick Moynihan, Midge Decter, Daniel Bell, Irving Kristol, and James Q. Wilson, who warned of "the limits of social reform," who drew on the neorealist traditions from which they emerged in the 1940s and 1950s to persuasively argue that good intentions often yielded bad results. The neoconservatives often acted out of the most unattractive motives, for instance, rage at unappreciative younger scholars and activists not willing to defer to those who had more than paid their dues. They positively *hated* the Sixties, especially its countercultural hedonism, its anti-intellectualism, its anti-anti-Communism, its rhetorical excesses. Their initial efforts were to introduce a note of caution to the expansion of the welfare state, to return to 1950s themes of paradox and irony, of a Niebuhrian awareness of human error. This was a genuine conservatism, one long called for by mainstream liberals like Lionel Trilling, who indeed was already contributing to its embryo.

However, the neoconservative achievement has been marred by the tendency of most of its voices to move from a tempered, tradition-based welfare statism mostly wary of "an excess of democracy" to a virtual surrender to the anti–welfare state, free-market views of those so-called paleoconservatives never interested in government for purposes other than morality, police action, and war. From a cautionary note that offered valuable insights and criticisms, too many neoconservatives, seduced by the Reagan victories, climbed aboard the laissez-faire wagon, forsaking all claims to being the voice of wisdom and tradition. In brief, they abandoned Freud for Norman Vincent Peale.

The neoconservatives provided the Right with intellectual legitimacy; they also created the narratives that branded efforts to address economic inequities as abysmal failures. Their move further right was driven more by culture wars than by public policy issues.

However, one must note that the belief that the War on Poverty failed, that Johnson's efforts to create a Great Society failed, is untrue. Indeed, as many policy analysts argue, there was no war on poverty but rather a series of, at best, skirmishes. The Economic Opportunity Act of 1964 focused on services rather than on income or employment. It was cheaper to provide community action programs, job training, legal services, and counseling to the poor than to create the kind of full-employment program that advisors such as Moynihan and radical critics like Michael Harrington proposed. The Office of Economic Opportunity (OEO) also fit "culture of poverty" arguments; it would help the poor, especially the children of the poor. If we couldn't "save" the adult poor caught in a self-destructive subculture, at least we could give their children a head start so that equality of opportunity could be realized.

The 1964 election gave LBJ the opportunity to act on his desire to be the next FDR, to expand, indeed to fulfill, the logic of the New Deal, to establish a comprehensive American welfare state. He delivered on health care, aid to education, beautification, child welfare; he had considerable success in reducing poverty, particularly among older Americans. But Johnson always tended toward rhetorical excess, for instance, why not build a *good* society before taking on the task of a *great* society? Why use military rhetoric when the OEO was so modestly funded? The War on Poverty started with a mere $800 million; it spent about $15 billion over its seven-year history. During that same period, the nation spent well over $100 billion, by some estimates as much as $300 billion, on the wars in Indochina. There was no war on poverty in any meaningful sense.

The most promising aspects of that effort were at the level of empowerment and prevention. OEO's "maximum partici-pation of the poor," despite its excesses, brought thousands of poor people for the first time into the political process, gave many local residents avenues that would take them to careers in public service. Community Legal Services was perhaps the most significant, providing, for the first time, lawyers to help poor people protect their rights—to welfare assistance, to par-ticular benefits, to be treated with dignity and respect. Pro-gressives should feel very proud of this legacy of the Sixties, a legacy worn down but not yet destroyed by the conservative attacks that began with Nixon and have yet to cease.

Conservatives believe that the public policies of the 1960s, especially those associated with the War on Poverty, created and expanded the underclass. Their argument is that the rad-ical and countercultural assaults on traditional values, espe-cially those relating to sex and drugs, created a cultural cli-mate of hedonism and irresponsibility. Conservatives charge that affluent rebels could always abandon their youthful decadence for suburbia and corporate jobs; poor people lacked such options. They paid the heaviest price for aban-doning traditional values.

Liberals and radicals have tended to define this critique as a form of blaming the victim, compounded by a character assassination of the presumed victimizer, often called "the new class" by conservatives. But all of the data in fact indicate an increase in cultural pathologies, for example, violent crimes, substance abuse, welfare dependency, family dysfunction. Why so?

Here I would agree with E. J. Dionne that we need to get past the liberal-versus-conservative narratives. Conservatives correctly point to the pathologies; they may be blaming the victim, but they are also observing social realities. Liberals correctly point to the policy inequities—the declining value of AFDC payments, the effects of deindustrialization on poorly educated people, especially African American men. Liberals are right that conservatives have *blamed* poor people and have been mean-spirited. The question is, What can be done to address the actual problems?

Reflecting on the legacies of the 1960s in terms of racial and poverty issues, we can at the very least recognize that our present ideological boxes, fashioned all too often by Sixties myths, preclude progress. Conservatives cannot be allowed to blame all of our woes, especially those pertaining to the underclass, on the War on Poverty and on the pernicious influence of countercultural hedonism. For the most part, people are poor because they don't have enough money to sustain a decent standard of living. One cannot begin to make sense of the plight of the poor, especially the black poor, without facing up to the impact of deindustrialization. If you're not heading toward college or to an apprenticed skilled trade, you're going nowhere in postmodern America; and if you're a man going nowhere, you're not likely to see yourself as the breadwinner, or as the cobreadwinner, of a family.

We need to move away from some of the ideological either/ ors of Sixties ideological battles—*either* culture of poverty *or* blaming the victim, *either* deindustrialization *or* family break- down. Too many black and white liberals have avoided and de- nied these realities for too long. In an affluent culture bom- barding all Americans with images of the good life, poverty can get inside a person. If that person is in a segregated neighbor- hood—crack infested, gang run, few dads (the Cabrini Greens and Taylor Homes of U.S. ghettoes)—whether one calls it a culture of poverty or prefers, as does Wilson, to see it as "ghetto-specific" behavior, life is diminished; many people be- come self-destructive. Opportunity, while essential, is not enough for such folks. They need a veritable crusade.

This crusade runs up against the antistatist skepticism now prevalent in our polity. Those interested in finally respond- ing to the Kerner Commission Report's challenge about two societies, one rich, one poor, one white, the other black, know what needs to be done:

1. We must direct enormous attention to schooling, to remedy the unacceptable loss of human potential associated with our worst, ghetto schools. We need to support the kinds of educational strategies associated with psychiatrist James Comer (alliances of administrators, teachers, parents, and students; compensation for dysfunctional families; inclusion of successful adults within the school system; safety; high standards) and Deborah Meier (small, face-to-face schools with smaller classrooms and hands-on teachers).

2. We need to "end welfare as we know it" by making work more attractive and welfare less so, through an ex- panded earned-income tax credit, a significantly higher min- imum wage, universal health care, child care, and educa- tional subsidies. It can't be done on the cheap, but the costs

we presently pay for low labor productivity, health care, crime, and personal insecurity are infinitely greater.

3. We need to address genuine issues of community security by focusing on violent crimes and moving away from our disastrous "war on drugs," which has filled our prisons to no purpose. William Mayer's study of public-opinion polls between the 1960s and the late 1980s indicates that while we have become infinitely more tolerant on issues of race and gender and strongly supportive of environmental protection, we have moved sharply to the right in matters of crime and punishment. This shift is only partially reducible to racism; much of it rests on actual, if often exaggerated, fears about personal and family security.

4. We need to accept as legitimate the conservative concerns about teen pregnancies and a welfare culture of dependency. But *most* poor people are either working but not making enough to manage or suffering from short-term crises like being laid off or becoming ill. These folks, who play by the rules, who work as hard or harder than a barrelful of arbitragers, need to be supported.

The most problematic legacy of the 1960s regarding race is how much our obsessions with it get in the way of progressive public policy. Black power as a form of identity politics, while explicable in terms of the deeply rooted racism of our society, has often served to obscure solutions to problems by playing the race card to deny obvious and troubling realities. Up until the mid-1960s, those committed to civil rights had the moral upper hand; they were the clear "good guys" by values, demeanor, goals.

But with Stokely and Rap Brown, strutting, martial Black Panthers, scowling Black Muslims, riots, violent crime, welfare rights militancy, Crown Heights, Tawana Brawley and Al

Sharpton, we enter a world most acutely, viciously, and brilliantly captured by conservatism's best writer, Tom Wolfe, and by Jim Sleeper, whose *The Closest of Strangers* tells the sad story of New York's racial politics. The decline in the moral authority of civil rights is part of what explains the conservative successes since Nixon. And it is part of understanding the end of the Sixties, which rested on the revival of political hope inspired by the example of African Americans and their white allies.

Certainly the more difficult economic issues Martin Luther King, Jr., began to stress by 1966 would not have been easily addressed and resolved, black power or no, identity politics or no. A genuine war on poverty required commitments in resources few Americans were willing to make, especially as the golden age of U.S. capitalism began to fade, as incomes stagnated or fell. But the New Politics of marginalizing working-class whites and being contemptuous of suburban Middle Americans, combined with an identity politics that made it easier to reduce race to a zero-sum game, doomed any efforts to alleviate poverty and other forms of human suffering. And this liberal and radical blindness made it that much easier for conservatives to surge forward with the argument that poverty wars actually *caused* poverty. Indeed, black power and radical activists were already half convinced!

One legacy of the 1960s should be the reenforcement of the belief that social movements set the parameters of social reforms. A host of recent studies highlight how broadly based the civil rights movement was. We need to focus on those strengths—that of a southern, church- and community-grounded movement of a people with a language, a set of metaphors, a framework of meaning and hope. The tragedy is how difficult it has been to transpose that southern black movement to northern—more accurately, urban—environments. But triumphs like those of the East Brooklyn Congegrations' Nehemiah Project—the construction of more than two thousand working-class homes, the reconstruction of a community through the leadership of the Reverend Johnny Ray Youngblood and St. Paul's Community Baptist Church—point to a strategy of possibilities. And we find other examples of such efforts in a variety of middle- and working-class communities, from San Antonio to Camden, New Jersey.

Such people participated in the Million Man March. Their responsiveness to the separatist, racist, and eccentric Louis Farrakhan rests, to a considerable degree, upon the ethical and political vacuum left by a black political leadership unable and unwilling to recognize that its own version of identity politics subverts the reinvention of a compelling vision of social reform. Such largely invisible black men—and women—hardworking folks, deserve better, both from their own leaders and from the nation.

A movement to reignite efforts to eliminate poverty in what remains a land of plenty must start with the rock of self-respect, human dignity, and a pragmatic, nonrhetorical commitment to social justice. Identity politics at its worst only reenforces victimhood, only gloats over signals of persistent bigotry, and finds more satisfaction in scoring points than in organizing people to improve their lives. A politics of envy and resentment, an ideology of essentialism simply insure that the truly disadvantaged will remain marginalized.

The Problem That Has a Name

When I teach the history of the second wave of feminism, I ask my students to tell me who was the first housewife. They are puzzled. Often, jokingly, one will assert, "Eve—Eve was the first housewife." The discussion quickly moves to definition—what is a housewife? Most understand that it is a woman who stays home, takes care of the kids, cleans the house, makes the dinners, does the laundry, and so on. They are surprised when I draw a gravestone on the board, write "R.I.P., Housewife, late 19th century—late 20th century." Sometimes I give foolishly exact dates to push the issue.

We then proceed to discuss the profound transformations associated with the industrial revolution that separated work from home. Since the neolithic revolution, most people in all parts of the world had been peasants, living in villages, defined by blood relations, within which the household (however defined, although characteristically patriarchal) was a combination of economy, school, and cultural transmission belt. The notion of hubby going off to work, whether to office or plant, is a nineteenth-century phenomenon. And as work separates from home, so do schooling and, increasingly, socialization. The housewife, affluent or not, has fewer children at lower risk, is caring for them for fewer years, and is isolated from the world of associated work in a way unknown to peasant women.

Compounding this developing isolation was the contradiction of U.S. democracy, especially as operationalized in public schooling. Even with prejudicial structures limiting women's access to educational opportunities, the country's public school and undergraduate systems were open to women; they were, for the most part, coed. So that at least among middle-class women, something approaching equal learning opportunities existed that then were closed off at the point of marriage and the family.

In 1963, Betty Friedan addressed this "problem that has no name." The problem of the educated, white, middle-class woman who sees her husband move into the world of enterprise or professional career while she remains stuck at home in a suburb, dependent on the automobile, devoting herself to her 2.2 children who increasingly bond with their friends, dedicating themselves to TV, movie, sports, and pop music culture, peer culture, *youth* culture. She's in her thirties, unhappy, taking it out on herself for not appreciating her good, devoted husband and her accomplished children, soon going off to college. What an ingrate! And much of psychotherapy tells her to get involved, do charity work, take a class in some craft—don't allow this "penis envy" to run your life!

Friedan pinpointed the contradiction facing mostly white, affluent women. Why educate them if they aren't given the opportunities to act on what they've learned? In an economy increasingly driven by brain and not brawn, the contradiction between the reactionary Fifties culture of domesticity and the desire of women to put their education to some use began to stretch beyond repair.

Younger women experienced these tensions within the framework of the Movement. As Sara Evans tells the story, the younger generation of second-wave feminists begins as civil rights and peace activists. Casey Hayden and Mary King, inspired by the examples of African American women they worked with, like Ella Baker and Ruby Doris Smith, hesitantly and most carefully, *anonymously* raised questions about the treatment of women within "the beloved community" of SNCC. The next year they were ridiculed by SDS's male leaders and proceeded to circulate a memo to female activists discussing sexual equality, linking it to the racial equality they had been fighting for. Indeed, as during the antislavery struggles of the antebellum period, the call for human rights for one group served as a model, an inspiration, a catalyst, and a source of resentment for other groups experiencing analogous mistreatment.

Within ten years, a thickly networked, vibrant women's

movement existed, constructed by several generations of feminists: those married, with children, and returning to work; those in college and single; lesbians oppressed by heterosexual biases; and lots of working women simply fed up with unequal treatment—airline employees, "stewardesses" like Dusty Roads and Nancy Collins, sick and tired of being infantilized, patronized, and limited in their career options. The transformation includes the creation of a literature, influential books, newsletters, new journals and magazines, the most obvious being *Ms.* in 1972; institutions devoted to women's interests, including clinics, legal services, reproductive rights organizations, labor unions, labor caucuses, political action committees, shelters, rape crisis centers, hotlines, bookstores—caucuses and coalitions in virtually all aspects of organizational life.

The second wave of this remarkable revolution in the relations between men and women, arguably the most profound and deepest of all human transformations, raised a series of questions that shook the patriarchal order to its roots. The issue that achieved the broadest consensus, precisely because it was the most grounded in U.S. traditions of liberty and equality, was the demand for equal rights, for the fullest opening of opportunities to women. It formed the essence of the agenda of the National Organization for Women (NOW), founded in 1966 and embodying what a number of commentators call liberal or equity feminism.

The baby-boomer segment among second-wave feminists did not believe that such traditional goals were sufficient; indeed, in some instances they found them bogus. At the heart of the more radical position, organized by veterans of civil rights and peace activism, was the argument that a formal, legal equality, while necessary, was not sufficient to address the underlying structures of what came to be called sexism. Here the slogan "The personal is political" takes center stage. Younger, more radical feminists were suspicious of a movement that limited itself to ameliorative reforms, leaving unchallenged the more institutionalized, socialized inequities. Their radicalism was to seek the roots of sexism in patriarchy, in the ways in which male domination permeated the most important institutions of the culture, most particularly the family.

Most of the Sixties generation of feminists were single, without children. Alice Echols's *Daring to Be Bad: Radical Feminism in America, 1967–1974* provides a marvelous sense of these early developments, particularly the radical cultural context within which women's liberationists interacted. When they began to reach out to each other, following the circulating of Casey Hayden and Mary King's 1965 memo, as they began to feel confirmed in their own experiences of being marginalized and disrespected by the male leadership within the movement, they started the consciousness-raising groups that played such a major role in confirming the ways in which one's personal and social life contained a politics of male chauvinism.

The questions that emerged from such groups and from the pioneer political formations, such as New York Radical Women, Redstockings, The Feminists, were radical in the most profound sense:

- What is a woman? What is a man? To what extent are differences biological? Cultural? What do we mean by masculine? Feminine?
- In seeking equality, can there be difference? Are differences reducible to socialization? Are women superior to men?

- To what extent is mothering natural? What is parenting?
- Who is responsible for child rearing? And how does it relate to career opportunity?
- Is the family inherently oppressive, sexist? What other ways can children be raised?
- Are men inherently sexist and therefore inevitably oppressive? Is heterosexual intercourse always rape?
- Is lesbianism, is a separatism the most logical means of reducing sexual oppression?

Women's liberation activists argued such questions with great vehemence in the late 1960s and early 1970s, indeed, *continue* to do so today. The divergent paths of second-wave feminism included the already noted liberal feminism, which tended toward the elimination of all barriers to opportunity and participation; a variety of socialist or political radical feminisms, which tended to see sexism as inextricably grounded in capitalist structures of exploitation and domination and consequently sought to integrate feminism, with Marxist categories; a radical feminism, which tended to argue that sexism and patriarchy were older and more deeply entrenched than capitalism and consequently sought to integrate Marxism, where applicable, to feminism; a cultural feminism, which tended to view sexism as the primary contradiction of human history and which therefore leaned toward a separatist, lesbian politics based on the notion that men were the enemy.

In rereading the literature of the birth of the women's liberation movement, I was struck by the ways in which the political and cultural visions of that period colored points of view in ways analogous to what occurred within the black power movement. For example, with the exception of the most liberal feminists of NOW, almost all participants assumed that capitalism had to go, that liberalism, bourgeois democracy were a fraud and a snare, and that the models for social transformation were the Third World revolutionary regimes of China, Cuba, and Vietnam. On the last point the separatists clearly took issue.

During the late Sixties and early Seventies, many movement activists trying to fend off feelings of despair (the war seemed endless; Nixon was in the White House and likely to be reelected, the movement had collapsed; countercultural visions of Woodstock Nation had crashed with Altamont and the deaths of rock stars) invested their hopes in utopian visions they associated with Maoism, with models of guerrilla warfare in which Regis Debray and Frantz Fanon were most influential theoretically and the Black Panthers the most politically exulted, with belief in what Che Guevara was calling "the new socialist man," a selfless, altruistic, cooperative being purged of the privatist individualism of bourgeois culture. The women's liberation movement bought into this utopian dream as heartily as other elements of the New Left.

Within this framework, one can understand some of the excesses, rhetorical and otherwise, of second-wave feminism: for example, Shulamith Firestone's argument in *The Dialectics of Sex* that artificial insemination would liberate women from the biology that kept them oppressed, or the totalitarian demands of some groups that individuals abandon lovers or husbands or makeup to demonstrate their ideological loyalties. It *was* a crazy time, its utopian frenzies belied by the rapidity with which the Movement was crashing in self-destruction.

It was in this period that identity politics was born. By identity politics, I mean a position that defines, restricts, and separates particular groups through an essentialist definition of their history, culture, and politics. Identity politics, in the case of women, assumes that there is a women's point of view or, more precisely, a feminist point of view. Identity politics tends toward a conditional tolerance of those within—all must toe the party line or risk excommunication as anti-feminist—and a hostility to those without, presupposed to be the adversary incapable of understanding the insider's essentialist position.

The Movement of the early and mid-1960s rested on a notion of a public interest, on a claim to a majoritarian, democratic politics. But as the Indochina War persisted, as the war came home in the form of ghetto riots, as the Great Society visions of Lyndon Johnson collapsed and Richard Nixon succeeded in forming his great silent majority coalition, many movement activists turned away from liberal and populist reforms, rejected democratic socialist views, and embraced a variety of positions, all of which *assumed* that the American people were hopelessly reactionary. They opted for chilling versions of utopian communism, vanguard militancies that embraced kamikaze tactics, or separatist—identity politics—agendas that denied the possibilities of a public interest.

What remains impressive is how much the women's liberation movement accomplished and set in motion despite such excesses. It is sometimes the case that extremists make moderate demands more acceptable, that Martin needed Malcolm as Betty Friedan required Ti-Grace Atkinson. But one of the problems of identity politics is that it seems to require a minimizing of the accomplishments, the extensive network of institutions and media, the astounding educational and career achievements of the women's movement. Identity politics *needs* to highlight victimization, *needs* to emphasize the power of its enemies, *needs* to maintain a war footing for its troops, a sense that, whatever progress has been achieved, outside of the oppressed group lie only treachery and betrayal. Without such a war footing, internal unity crumbles and polarities between inside and outside soften and blur. Unfortunately, in these times of Contracts with (and on) America, it is not particularly difficult to document charges of backlash and betrayal. Enemies abound; reaction exists.

Christina Hoff Sommers has gotten a lot of mileage out of muckraking the self-interested and problematic claims of many feminists, for instance, claims about the number of anorexia nervosa deaths among women, claims about the extent of low self-esteem among teenage girls, claims about gender bias in schools, claims about Super Bowl–induced violence against women. Daphne Patai and Noretta Koertge have provided what they call "cautionary tales from the strange world of women's studies," accounts of ideology reigning over science, of the personal as the political imposing a severe form of political correctness. Perhaps most disturbing in *Professing Feminism* is that most of the tales, told by feminists alienated from women's studies programs, are anonymous.

How is one to relate such criticisms, and one might add those of Jean Bethke Elshtain, Wendy Kaminer, and Elizabeth Fox-Genovese, to the kinds of arguments made by Susan Faludi in *Backlash,* a highly successful polemic arguing that women and feminism have been and remain under attack, have been losing ground to a reactionary sexism coming in both liberal and conservative molds? Are we going forward or backward? As Gregg Easterbrook asserts regarding the environment, have we exaggerated defeat and loss, snatched defeat from the jaws of victory?

The evidence regarding women is significantly stronger than that addressing African Americans, although in both instances the decline associated with living in or close to poverty hits women and minorities particularly hard. Fox-Genovese, among others, argues that the individualist, middle-class biases of the women's movement have led it away from a focus on the working class and the poor. However, the Faludi thesis of erosion and defeat seems belied by the relevant data concerning gender progress. That there is sexism in our schools is indisputable; that it is growing seems open to, at the least, some skepticism. That schoolgirls are less confident than schoolboys may be a partial truth, but it needs to come to grips with complementary tensions experienced by the boys and with the striking outcomes correlated with gender. Women are more likely to attend and graduate from college than men. They earn more master's degrees than men. In 1970, women earned only 6 percent of professional degrees; by 1991 they earned 39 percent, and that percentage continues to rise. In twenty years women's share of doctoral degrees has risen from 14 percent to 39 percent, of medical degrees from 8 percent to 36 percent. Women as of 1993 made up 42 percent of medical students, 40 percent of law students, and 32 percent of dental students. Just twenty years ago, these percentages were less than 10 percent, in dentistry a mere 1 percent.

This is not to suggest we've achieved feminist heaven. Critics such as Sommers minimize the very real and persistent indices of gender bias and sexual discrimination, especially among poor women. They tend to pick out the most outrageous voices and embarrassing moments, ignoring the steady, persistent efforts of most feminists to continue the march toward equality and fairness. But the point should be well taken; there seems to be a tendency to dwell on the negatives, even to the point of considerable distortion of what surely must be defined as progress.

African American and feminist identity politics rest on the collapse of both liberal and radical visions: the Great Society welfare state model Lyndon Johnson sought to complete and the beloved community, participatory democracy associated with SNCC and SDS new leftists. Identity politics shares with New—and Old—Left visions a tendency to reduce all ideas to ideology, to hold to a reductionist notion of totality, to assume that not only the personal but the cultural and the social and the aesthetic are all political, that is, politically determined by the interests of groups. In this sense the emergence of postmodernism—the influence of Michel Foucault, the reduction of knowledge to power and domination—rests on the Marxist tradition. The privileged position of the proletariat, or at least of its designated representatives, is replaced by the essentialism of historically oppressed groups. Thus we have a strange alliance of the most sophisticated sociology of knowledge and literary criticism (Foucault, Jacques Derrida) with a victims' essentialism (Molefi Asante, Catherine MacKinnon). It's a cynical alliance with no hopes of reconstructing a vision of a shared universe, of a democratic community.

As Jean Bethke Elshtain soberly notes, it makes no sense to expect academics to bravely take on what has come to be called political correctness. She concludes, agreeing with Russell Jacoby, "Academics tend to swim in schools like fishes." But considerable grounds for optimism remain. First and foremost, there are loads of intellectuals, writers, even academics resistant to identity politics and political correctness.

One of the most impressive consequences of the Sixties racial and gender revolutions is the richness and variety of voices that we hear now and that must resound into the future. It's increasingly impossible for essentialist thinkers to make claims for there being an African American or a woman's point of view. Who do we mean? Gerald Early? Patricia Williams? Derrick Bell? Henry Louis Gates? Toni Morrison? Stanley Crouch? Thomas Sowell? Michelle Wallace? John Wideman? Albert Murray? Julius Lester? Sister Souljah? Leon Higginbotham? Lani Guinier? Kwami Anthony Appiah? Ron Karenga? Do we mean Camille Paglia or Andrea Dworkin? Ellen Willis? Marilyn French? Katie Roiphe? bell hooks? Katha Pollitt? Robin Morgan? Nancy Chodorow? Carol Gilligan? Mary Daly? Adrienne Rich?

This richness of voices offers hope that we can move away from an identity politics. It must be emphasized that a goodly measure of the charges against political correctness rests on the discomfort experienced by the narrow-minded and the fearful at the cultural and social transformations of the past thirty or so years. Opposing bigotry, criticizing sexual innuendos or racial jokes are forms of political correctness that are now the mainstream common sense and civility—and fortunately so. Too many conservatives simply want their own version of political correctness, perhaps as imposed by the Christian Coalition or the National Rifle Association (NRA). But progressives have too easily allowed the Right to make a persuasive case about political correctness, particularly on college campuses plagued by both essentialist and postmodern denials of freedom of expression.

One of the saddest and most maddening aspects of the political correctness controversy has been the reversal of roles, with conservatives defending and radicals opposing free speech. The conservative hypocrisy is glaring—those who have applauded Joe McCarthy, who seek required prayer in the schools, who censure pornography and obscenity, who blast the ACLU become the ardent defenders of the rights of students. What's remarkable is that campus radicals have not

zeroed in on this demagogy. In part that's because the prevailing winds of identity politics have contempt for notions
of the marketplace of ideas and the pursuit of truth. If knowledge is simply power, if ideas are simply instruments of domination, then one logically ends with Mao, the NRA, and
Stanley Fish agreeing that power grows out of the barrel of a
gun!

Identity politics follows from the collapse of the Sixties
movements. It is a politics of victims precisely because it ax-
iomatically denies a shared politics, a belief in a potentially
common, American interest. And it seems to *need* a despondent to apocalyptic vision, a bleak forecast of possibilities. Indeed there is much to sustain such despair, especially among
African Americans. Racism runs very deep. Sexism in many
ways runs deeper. But it remains striking how little recognition is accorded the extraordinary gains of the past thirty years.

I believe that for those gains to be affirmed, the advocates
of identity politics—minorities, women, environmentalists—
would have to come to grips with their ambivalence about
those working- and middle-class, mostly suburban Americans who have been absorbing, little by little, sometimes at
an agonizing snail's pace, with backsliding and backlashes,
the multicultural challenges raised most sharply and bravely
by the movements associated with the 1960s. Old Left, New
Left, and identity politics share a stereotyping of the middle-
class mainstream, especially its suburban core. It's a contempt repaid in triplicate with devastating consequences to
the possibilities of a democratic political movement. To
move beyond identity politics, we will have to imagine a democratic political movement that includes Middle America.

Lastly, intertwined with those remarkable gains have been
terrible declines of the ability of many Americans, especially

those without college degrees, including many Middle Americans, to maintain a secure life. Identity politics is a symptom but, worse, a snare; it divides precisely those groups needing to coalesce against the rising gap between rich and poor, against the fragility of working- and middle-class standards of living. The decline of trade union participation rests on the increasing leverage of global corporations operating in a global market; identity politics has not created this loss of popular power, but it, alas, has played a significant role in making it more difficult for working people to find common ground. As a result, what Michael Lind calls the invisibility of the "overclass," those at the top whose share of national wealth keeps increasing, rests in part on the pervasiveness of identity politics.

6

Another Sixties: The New Right

When the tumult of the Sixties finally subsided, and
the dust settled, the New Left suffered decline, albeit
with powerful influence on a host of movements. But
one could argue that history belongs more to those
who rallied to Goldwater in 1964, responded to
George Wallace's appeal to white backlash, and built
the counterestablishment that spawned the Reagan
revolution, which remains alive, even dominant, into
the Nineties under the congressional leadership of
Newt Gingrich and his mostly boomer freshman
class of '94.

As late as the mid-1950s there wasn't yet a consensus that conservatism defined a right-wing movement. Only with the emergence of Buckley's *National Review* in 1955 did conservatives consistently
call themselves conservatives. Buckley's journal
boasted thirty thousand readers in 1960, sixty thou-

sand by 1964, and more than one hundred thousand by 1969. He was central as well to the founding of the Young Americans for Freedom (YAF) in 1960, whose mostly student membership reached seventy thousand. Who were these students? They seem to have been both less affluent, more vocationally driven, and more Roman Catholic than those attracted to SDS.

I want to suggest the range of New Right baby boomers through a series of portraits. Those selected reflect significant stories and themes that I believe offer insight into the success of a revived Right into the Seventies and the Eighties, but they by no means reflect a statistical sample of Sixties-generation conservatives. Most of all, they tell the kinds of stories we all need to hear if we are finally to come to grips with the still omnipresent 1960s.

New Right baby-boomer stories can be examined within a set of polarities. One is the extent to which a Sixties conservative was touched by the political or cultural radicalism of that decade. David Stockman, for example, flirted with SDS; Richard Cheney seems to have been totally unaffected by Sixties challenges, despite studying at a very epicenter of eruption—the University of Wisconsin campus at Madison. Another issue is the impact of cultural change. Cheney and Elliot Abrams never felt the attractions of Woodstock Nation; indeed both seem to have moved into traditional adult roles before completing college. On the other hand, conservatives like Lee Atwater, Bill Bennett, and P. J. O'Rourke present themselves as devoted rock 'n' rollers, hardly likely to thrill to more favored GOP entertainers like Bob Hope or Wayne Newton. Let me suggest a typology for conservative baby boomers.

Traditionalists: Dick Cheney and James Webb

In 1969, Dick Cheney was a graduate student at the University of Wisconsin, the setting for the Sixties documentary "The War at Home." On a campus famous for its tolerance of political dissent, home to the New Left journal *Studies on the Left,* to radical historians such as William Appleman Williams and Harvey Goldberg, to a powerful movement against the Vietnam War that targeted university complicity in the war effort with protests against the napalm-producing Dow Chemical Company—on such a campus, Dick Cheney began his career as a rock-solid conservative politician.

Cheney, born in 1943, came out of Caspar, Wyoming, which his high school sweetheart Lynn describes as an "*American Graffiti* kind of place" where "the big thing was to drive cars up and down, and go from one root beer stand to another." But young Dick Cheney never so indulged: "He worked; he always had a job. He read a lot." One should add that this youthful workaholic was no nerd; he captained the football team and was an avid outdoorsman.

Cheney went off to Yale on a scholarship but did poorly and dropped out after three semesters. He returned to his roots, graduating from the University of Wyoming, marrying Lynn, and proceeding to Madison for a master's in political science. His key breakthrough was a one-year internship in the Washington office of a local congressman, where he impressed the up-and-coming Donald Rumsfeld. Cheney moved with Rumsfeld from the Office of Economic Opportunity staff to first Nixon's and then Ford's staff, where, when Rumsfeld became defense secretary, Cheney was promoted to chief of staff. He was thirty-four. When Carter defeated Ford, Cheney, having already suffered the first of three heart attacks, successfully ran for Congress from his home district in Wyoming. As a six-term congressman, Cheney was consistently conservative, hard-line on defense, committed to Contra aid and to Star Wars.

What is intriguing about this utterly uncharismatic, efficient, hawkish former defense secretary is the fact that he never served in the armed forces. He says that he was generally supportive of the Vietnam War and opposed to the demonstrators. But his hawkishness didn't lead him to volunteer; instead, he accepted student deferments that allowed him to avoid military service. All Cheney will say is, "As did most other Americans, I watched the war from afar." There remains something odd about this hard-line Cold Warrior's evasion of what would seem to be his patriotic duty.

One must note that, by conventional estimate, Cheney is not a baby boomer. Of course neither are most of the founders of SDS, the New Left initiators of second-wave feminism, or the leading voices among the countercultural hippies. Cheney is a war baby, like Dick Darman, Newt Gingrich, and the CIA's Robert Gates. Pat Caddell's expanded framework for baby boomers, which includes those born during World War II, seems most appropriate here.

By contrast, in an early chapter of his Vietnam novel *Fields of Fire,* James Webb takes a few jabs at Harvard students who found a variety of ways to avoid military service during the Vietnam era. He prefaces a chapter with a general's comments to a journalist on those who did and did not serve: "And who are the young men we are asking to go into action against such solid odds? You've met them. You know. They are the best we have. But they are not McNamara's sons, or Bundy's. I doubt they're yours. And they know they're at the end of the pipeline. That no one cares. They know."

Webb, a 1968 Annapolis graduate, is proud of descending from a line of southerners who had fought in virtually every American war, beginning with the American Revolution and including Confederate service during the Civil War. He served in Vietnam in 1969 as a marine rifle-company commander, earning a Navy Cross (for wounds he suffered while shielding one of his men from a grenade explosion), a Silver Star, two Bronze Stars, and two Purple Hearts. In brief, James Webb was a war hero.

Webb defends the U.S. involvement in Vietnam but argues that "the military was forced to pay a human cost for the country's caution and then paid again with its prestige when some labelled the inevitable results of such limited activity 'military incompetence'." About himself, he states, "In my mind, I am a writer. In my heart, I am a soldier, and I always will be."

Webb is an intriguing figure precisely because of the ways in which he differs from Cheney—and from Dan Quayle. He has always been a straight shooter, a ramrod soldier-intellectual willing to speak unpleasant truths. His Vietnam novels and articles savage not only peaceniks, whom he blames for upwards of ten thousand American deaths in Vietnam, but also arrogant marine officers whose ineptness put at risk the lives of the grunts Webb commanded and respected. There is a populist core to Jim Webb, a deep allegiance to everyday virtues, to the values he associates with his own Missouri, dirt-farm roots: "You must never violate your loyalty if you wished to survive the judgment of the ages. If nothing ever works out all the way, and if all things change, what's left? Your family and your friends and your values, that's what's left. And your duty to them. . . . They are the only important thing in life." Webb differs from both Cheney and Quayle not only in his Vietnam service but in the ways in which his politics has been driven, in part, by a conservative populist reaction to and resentment about the movements of the 1960s, defined as permissive, hedonistic, hypocritical, and, most of all, elitist. Of equal note is that iconoclasts like Webb seem blind to the upper-crust hypocrisies of their fellow conservatives.

For example, in *Fields of Fire*, Webb uses Harvard as an emblem of antiwar selfishness, lack of patriotism, and cowardice. In closing scenes he has the father of a returning vet turn a draft evader over to the police and then concludes the novel with the now chastened Harvard vet being harassed by snotty student radicals after calling them on their hypocrisies.

Webb stands as somewhat of a contrary personality, attractive in his courage, problematical in his choices. He got in a heap of trouble, for example, condemning the integration of women into the armed forces; he initially condemned Maya Lin's Vietnam Memorial as "a mass grave," an insult to Vietnam veterans; he was a critic of George Bush's Persian Gulf policies. In many ways, Webb is a more attractive version of at least the manufactured mythos of Oliver North, his contemporary at Annapolis.

Whereas in North one senses an underlying immaturity, a compensatory bravado, in Jim Webb one is persuaded of a steely, stubborn, virtuous, if difficult, core. In brief, independent of ideology, Webb commands respect. His portraits of peaceniks, feminists, liberals are often drawn one-dimensionally, but his loyalty to those who fought in the front lines in Vietnam, his loyalty to those of the past, present, and future who resonate to his mountaineer brand of patriotism, is powerfully evoked.

Traditionalists Obsessed with the Sixties:
Elliot Abrams and William Kristol

Concerning Elliot Abrams, there can be no neutrality. His is a high-wire ideological act within which are no subtleties, no maybes—to put a twist on a Sixties cliché, you're either part of the problem or part of the solution. Abrams grew up in a New York, Jewish, liberal Democratic household. Moreover, he was educated at the progressive Elizabeth Irwin High School, where the range of commitment stretched from beat cool to ADA (Americans for Democratic Action) liberalism, from Jack Kerouac to Adlai Stevenson, with considerable challenge from various contentious Marxist voices. Abrams bought into the political passions but kept his distance from all forms of cultural deviance. In this sense he was a true and loyal son of his rather strict parents.

One of his Harvard roommates declares, "Elliott was completely out of sympathy with the cultural tone of the Sixties. He was the only person I ever met who looked more comfortable in a brand-new pair of Levis than worn-out ones." Another roommate recalls him as "basically happy, well-adjusted, and unalienated. . . . He had good relations with his family and was always far more oriented to success, including monetary, than anyone else we knew." Abrams lived at Adams House, which had become a left-wing center; he became a leader among the anti–New Left, anti-Communist enclave, a mix of Social Democrats, liberals, and conservatives. Even within this culturally conservative group, he stood out as "a metaphor for the parents everybody had left behind. He seemed immunized against the common collegiate attractions of sex, drugs, and rock 'n' roll." Abrams flirted with some aspects of Sixties politics, including criticisms of the

Vietnam War and of local police abuses, but his heart was always more mainstream, as witness his support for Hubert Humphrey in the 1968 presidential campaign.

Abrams personifies those baby boomers fundamentally and negatively shaped by the Sixties rebellions, of a different order from old-fashioned ramrods like Webb. Several of them, like Carl Gershman, come out of the Old Left, anti-Communist culture. They resonate to Depression-era labor and campus wars between Communists and Socialists. Many of them began with a mistrust of what they perceived as left utopianism. They were often particularly incensed at the refusal of New Left activists to recognize the need to refuse collaboration with Communists. They remained loyal to organized labor and found even more baffling the New Left flirtation with the hippie counterculture. It seemed particularly irresponsible. Abrams, for example, felt revulsion at the mindlessness, the hedonism of so much of that era; one friend suggests that Abrams is still living in confrontation with the Sixties, still shaped by the images of New Left zealotry and campus enragés.

William Kristol shares with Abrams what might be called the "anti–red diaper baby syndrome". His father, Irving, and his mother, the historian Gertrude Himmelfarb, frame his experiences. Unlike Abrams, he was always a Vietnam hawk; at Harvard in the early Seventies he wore a Spiro Agnew sweatshirt. Kristol condemned those "cocksure radicals who thought they were the smartest generation ever and that none of the traditions were worth preserving." And he was untouched by the cultural transformations, except in opposition—short hair, no drugs, no rock 'n' roll.

Kristol is particularly interesting insofar as he has guided both Quayles in their intragenerational polemics, Dan's *Murphy Brown* attack and Marilyn's convention speech. To this generationally rooted element in the conservative movement, the Sixties is fair game. It is the core of the cultural war for hegemony—and it is a war whose early battles occurred during the 1960s, on campuses. Abrams and Kristol represent a relatively small but highly influential segment of New Right baby boomers; they were on the outside from the start, truly their parents' children, as Bob Dylan might say, "forever old." In contrast stand those more a part of the Sixties cultural transformations, who remain "forever young."

New Right Sixties Generation:
Peggy Noonan, Lee Atwater, and Bill Bennett

Peggy Noonan is an Irish Catholic baby boomer raised in the same Massapequa, Long Island, suburb as Ron Kovic, whose story is told in *Born on the Fourth of July*. Noonan's story in *What I Saw at the Revolution* offers the most significant variation on generational change:

> I come from people who were part of the fruits of the FDR realignment—the Catholics of the big cities who fully adhered to the Democratic Party in the Thirties and forties and never meant to let go—and became myself part of the quiet realignment of the eighties, in which what had seemed in my youth the party of rich dullards became, almost in spite of itself, the party of the people. . . . [this book] is about me and what led me to be the first of my family to become that dread thing—a Republican.

Noonan describes her Massapequa lower-middle-class suburb as a world where "not everything is possible, you can't have everything, and that's not bad, that's life. . . . Show respect, love your country, stop complaining!"

Noonan airbrushes out the dark side of the Fifties, including McCarthyism, racism, and the oppressiveness of postwar gender politics. But at the same time, her depiction of a suburban-dominated landscape captures, indeed embodies, central myths in the rightward migration of European immigrant-stock people. Noonan tells of her family's love affair with Jack Kennedy, who "opened the doors of American glamor to the working class," then delivers a double-edged compliment to the Democrats who, she says, "made us aware of how it is for people who don't have much, and that was good. But the culture of resentment the Democrats churned up in an effort to create consensus helped build a burgeoning underclass with a bitter sense of entitlement—which wasn't good at all. Still, it's hard not to like the party that at least noticed."

A disinterested student in high school, Noonan attended Fairleigh Dickinson University part-time for two years while working at Aetna Insurance in Newark, before enrolling on a full-time basis. Noonan became editor of her college newspaper and stayed safely mainstream: "It was Jersey, and we were first-in-our-family college students, and we were working a job and studying and partying, and only rich kids wanted to occupy a dean's office, normal kids just wanted to not get called on the carpet there." Noonan's concept of "normal kids" tilts more toward the middle than the working class. For example, of the Vietnam War, she admits, "The war didn't affect me in a direct way. I lost no one." Like the silent-majority baby boomers I've studied, Noonan lived at a distance from the realities of black and Hispanic public school and white working-class parochial school graduates and dropouts who served and died in Vietnam.

Noonan's story is a paradigm of New Right myth making.

She speaks of "the moment I wasn't of the Left," during a 1971 bus ride to a Washington antiwar demonstration. She saw "contempt for the nineteen-year-old boys who were carrying guns in the war or in the Guard. . . . It was understood that they were undereducated, and somewhat crude. There was contempt for America." Noonan asked herself, "What am I doing with these people?" and shouted, at least to herself, "Get me off this bus!"

Note that Noonan is embracing grunts who she admittedly doesn't know personally and is concentrating her rage against "their more advantaged brothers and sisters (who) were back home giving interviews to Eric Severeid on the Concord Bridge . . . the professionals and news producers and opinion leaders of the baby-boom generation." Off the hook are those like herself who managed to avoid both the war and the protests. Her new-class analysis argues that "the characters they invent on *thirtysomething* and *L.A. Law* will never admit that they were wrong not to oppose Communist tyranny in Vietnam." Her version of *The Big Chill* is the "chronic unease" and guilt among those boomers whose antiwar actions "helped produce the boat people, the Cambodian holocaust, a gulag called Vietnam, and an untold increase in horror for the people of that part of the planet."

Most interesting is Noonan's emphasis on generational re-alignment: "Up on the Hill or at the White House the young rough-looking guy from the state school is probably either a Republican or a conservative, and the snooty guy with a thank you for not smoking sign on his tidy little desk is a Democrat." She is fully aware that "movement conservatives" are "a bunch of creepy little men with creepy little beards who need something to seethe on"; nevertheless Noonan sees hope in her generation of new rightists:

> I know of almost no Republicans beyond middle age who un-
> derstand this, but the younger ones get it. Someone could gal-
> vanize the party by making a passionate speech that says,
> "This is the future—you're a working-class party, the party of
> the people who are learning to speak English for the first
> time." Redefine why we're Republicans—freedom and oppor-
> tunity connect with the desires of the poor and just-barely-
> making it, which are the same as those in the middle and the
> upper-middle. We blame it on the blacks that they allowed
> themselves to be bought by the Democratic Party but at least
> the Democrats wanted them, at least they cared.

Sounding like a right-wing Saul Alinsky, Noonan preaches,
"The conservatives, in the sixties and seventies, didn't go into
the churches, to the neighborhood gathering places, and
make their case with fire." In 1994 we saw a newer, more
baby-boom crew of Republican conservatives making and
winning such a case.

Noonan has an essentially cinematic vision of America,
which allows her to desire not so much a movie actor as president, but rather a president as movie actor. Hear her on Reagan: "In the fifties and early sixties . . . he was going from
plant to plant for GE, shooting the breeze with the workers
in the cafeteria, the guys on the line telling him what they
thought. More than any President since Jackson, he spent the
years before power, with people, the normal people of this
country." No wonder she claims, "All of us as adults now,
that's how we get our sense of our country, from the movies.
All of us, including him." Noonan crafts movie scripts; she
doesn't seem to read much history.

It would be easy but foolish to write Peggy Noonan off
as a lightweight. For better and worse, there is weight, substance, and power in her vision and her myth, as damaging

and absurd as it often is. Noonan understands, for example, the dangers of fanaticism: "Beware the politically obsessed. They are often bright and interesting, but they have something missing in their natures; there is a hole, an empty place, and they use politics to fill it up." Such truths swing left and right. She speaks of two kinds of activists, "those who are impelled by love, and those who get their energy from hate," concluding that the haters "cannot engage in honorable debate because they cannot see the honor of the other side."

The recent works by the Edsalls and Dionne suggest the critical importance of the disaffection of Middle America from the New Deal tradition. At the moment of Peggy Noonan's Republican apostacy, her mother chastised, "My father always said, 'stick with the Democrats. They're the party of the working man.'" Noonan replied, "When grandpa said that, it was true. It's not anymore." Peggy Noonan, a Sixties-generation conservative, part of what she calls "the up-and-coming constituency of young ethnic Catholics," uncomfortable with country club Republicanism, places her faith in the supply-side gospel that "growth is all," adding that "growth doesn't come from noblesse oblige, thank you very much." A portrait of GOP strategist Mary Matalin would reveal similar characteristics and have analogous significance; such ethnic women are part of the conservative Republican success in presenting themselves as populists and revolutionaries.

Along with Noonan, Lee Atwater is the most important kind of conservative baby boomer. Whereas Noonan represents the newly suburban Reagan Democrats, the northern, immigrant-stock ethnics, Atwater is a good old boy southerner and a fraternity boy cutup who reflects the ways in which Sixties liberation, the sex, drugs, and rock 'n' roll trinity, have often led to quite conservative ends.

Atwater is "a street-fighting . . . anti-Establishment man from the git-go," according to David Remnick. Like Noonan, Atwater speaks for the right-wing populism so much at the heart and soul of conservative successes since the Seventies. As a senior in high school, he ran his first successful campaign for a friend seeking the student government presidency: "I made up a whole lot of phony issues for him to run on. You can imagine: free beer on tap in the cafeteria, unlimited cuts, no grades less than Bs. We made up a whole list of credentials, including the fact that Yon had led an Arctic expedition and was the winner of the International Hairy Legs Contest."

Of course, his boy won.

Atwater is the conservative most focused on generational issues. He identifies himself strongly, passionately with *his* version of the Sixties. While in high school, he had a white soul band, the Upsetter's Review, which had some local success playing Motown and the likes of Otis Redding and Wilson Pickett. His folks persuaded him to go to college instead of hitting the road with the band. There, at local Newberry College, while still a rock 'n' roll animal, he found his primary passion in politics, first with a summer internship in Strom Thurmond's Washington office. Atwater became active in College Republicans, rose to state chair, and then went on to the national office before joining the GOP consulting firm of Black, Manafort & Stone.

Atwater *is* a conservative, a believer in Right to Life, free-market economics, anti-Communism. But he is mostly committed to winning, to the chase, to the sheer joy of political battle. In this sense, he is more scoundrel than ideologue, more the southern rascal—he admires Huey Long—than the Klansman. He can use the race issue for political purposes at the same time that he can wax enthusiastically about the African American contribution of the blues.

Most of all, Atwater offers hints of *M*A*S*H** crossed with *Porky's*, of the good old boy cum fraternity boy cum iconoclast. Sixties activists, Left and Right, challenged authority of all types; they helped to break down patterns of deference and tradition. They were rebelling against men in gray-flannel suits, organization men, a bureaucratic, white-collar environment that seemed to operate as if there was no longer such a thing as the human body. Such was their attraction to rock 'n' roll, the reassertion of the body, of movement and sexuality; they celebrated the moment, humor, spontaneity, trying to goose an uptight system. But in several ways, they were extending what some observers called "the fun morality." They were advancing a culture of abundance. Atwater personifies a fun morality, a liberation from restraint that the Sixties encouraged, but without the social conscience, the social agenda associated with the Left. He embodies the "flight from commitment" Barbara Ehrenreich associated with both the beats and the *Playboy* philsophy, which shaped much of the male-defined counterculture of the Sixties. To Atwater, "it's all a gas . . . the whole deal," "the whole phantasmagoria of politics and TV rock 'n' roll and baby-boom demographics." You can bet, if he had still been alive, he would have understood far better than World War II veterans Bush and Jim Baker the political importance of Bill Clinton's sax performance on Arsenio and the "Rock the Vote" campaign of MTV. Newt Gingrich certainly did in his remarkable efforts to both claim and trash the 1960s.

Another voice who both affirms and critiques the Sixties is Bill Bennett. Bennett combines aspects of several kinds of conservative baby boomers; in some ways he seems more like the progeny of neoconservative veterans of Old Left wars—Elliot Abrams, Irving Kristol—even though his own family background is Catholic and mainstream. Bennett, like Noonan and Atwater, carries populist passions, resentments at the wealthy nurtured by his divorced mother. Although he went to elite Williams College, he had to wait tables and spend summers hauling furniture to cover his costs. He juxtaposes his own Middle American experiences with what he caricatures as a New Left elite.

Bennett most reflects the transformation of the liberal into, first, a neoconservative, and then a conservative. Michael Massing claims there are two Bill Bennetts—one passionate, accessible, thoughtful; the other intolerant, combative, Nixonian. There is another dualism. Bennett, a staunch pro–civil rights liberal at Williams, was attracted to SDS but was persuaded by his older brother, Robert, that SDS membership might not look good on future resumés. This additional dualism juxtaposes idealism with ambition.

Bennett, an offensive tackle, "a lover of Aristotle and rock 'n' roll," studied under John Silber at Texas, where he stayed clear of campus politics. When he taught philosophy at Southern Mississippi in 1967–1968, he was still a liberal, publicly championing the message and the legacy of Martin Luther King, Jr.

Bennett's dramatic moment, comparable to Noonan's Washington bus ride, occurred in 1970 when he was attending Harvard Law School. There he was dormitory proctor to a black freshman pre-med student who wanted to switch to sociology. Bennett, convinced that the student was merely responding to peer pressures, refused to sign off on the change in major. An argument began that continued into the Harvard dining room. "I followed him to his table, and he said,

'You can't sit here,' and I said, 'Why not?' and he said, 'It's just for blacks.' And I said, 'That's a lot of junk. I heard that in Mississippi, and now I'm hearing it at Harvard.'" Bennett, already alienated by what he perceived as the anti-Americanism of student protesters and by black power activists, became a neoconservative, "his intellectual hero" became Irving Kristol, and he went off to work for John Silber at Boston University.

In 1982, when he was chosen to head the National Endowment of the Humanities, he was accurately perceived as the neoconservative option to the more right-wing M. E. Bradford of the University of Dallas. But by 1986, by then secretary of education, he had more than built his bridges to the right wing of the conservative movement.

Bennett, who won a lottery date with Janis Joplin in his college years, despite his ferocious Sixties bashing identifies himself as a rock 'n' roller. After explaining to his limo driver how to identify a Neil Sedaka song, he proclaimed, "That's Manfred Mann—'Do Wah Diddy', 'Hey, Cleve,' he called out, 'Ever know a Secretary of Education who knew rock 'n' roll before?'" A staunch polemicist against cultural relativism, Bennett nevertheless tempers his admiration for Allen Bloom: "I hate that prissy crap where he's anti–rock 'n' roll."

Bennett speaks of his resentments at privilege: "I really dislike snobs, pretentious people who mistreat people who have to work for them. I hate them." It is here that Bennett stands with the right-wing populism that has so driven the generational aspects of New Right success—the attacks on the new class, on the cultural elite, although virtually never on the Fortune 500. Bennett, whom his former mentor John Silber now castigates as "the Sorcerer's Apprentice" for his ruthless opportunism, sees himself as a champion of old liberal values and everyday people against the phonies and snobs. He has a sharp eye for left-of-center hypocrisies; none for his own. He has become a "virtuecrat" at odds with his party's promiscuous celebration of individualism and market supremacy and a critic of some of its anti-immigrant nativism. But he seems classically Sixtyish in not being able to settle down, to stick to a task, to run for office; in this regard he resembles Jesse Jackson.

New Left–to–New Right Sixties Generation: David Stockman, David Horowitz, Peter Collier, and Ron Radosh

David Stockman was caught up in the Barry Goldwater campaign of 1964, inspired, as he writes in *The Triumph of Politics,* by "the truths of Christianity and Republicanism" of his grandfather, a midwestern supporter of the far right Liberty Lobby. But he then went off to college where he fell "into the clutches of campus radicalism," taking up "Marxism and America-hating." Always melodramatic, Stockman concludes, "Liberal professors and anti-war agitators shattered everything I believed in." But "when the radicals turned violent," he adds, "I finally saw the light." The young David Stockman who had flirted with Students for a Democratic Society at Michigan State "discovered that the left was inherently totalitarian." Interestingly, Stockman, who says he found intellectual nourishment from the ideas of Reinhold Neibuhr and Walter Lippmann, and sponsorship from Daniel Patrick Moynihan, David Broder, and John Anderson—centrists all—calls himself "a radical ideologue." The road from SDS to the supply side of town did not seem so long.

Most striking are the ways in which Stockman defines his

adversaries during his tenure as Ronald Reagan's Director of the Office of Management and Budget. His sounds remarkably similar to the voices in which new leftists once excoriated liberal Democrats—corporate liberals—unwilling to confront the inherent contradictions of capitalism. Stockman's new truth came from a free-market ideology every bit as passionate and abstract as the Frankfurt School of neo-Marxism. He became "a disciple of F. A. Hayek," and, through the influence of Jack Kemp, read Jude Wanniski's *Way the World Works,* which, he tells, "hit me with the force of revelation." Notice how he describes this New Right rebirth: "It was exciting. Our ideas could change history. For the first time since my shaggy-haired days in the East Lansing coffee house, I began to feel as if I was part of a movement. My revolutionary fires had been rekindled once again."

The analogies between New Left and New Right, between left anarchism and right libertarianism, the patterns of crossover and overlap in the careers of Garry Wills, Murray Rothbard, Karl Hess, Ron Radosh have yet to be adequately explored. Minimally, one notices the utopian fervor, the sense of belonging to what both camps glowingly call a movement. When Stockman agreed to an *Atlantic* interview with William Greider, he offered this explanation—"Like me, he was anti-political." To both New Left and New Right, authenticity, commitment, a beloved community stand in contrast to Weber's ethic of responsibility, the world of politics and, therefore, compromise. Consider 1964—the Goldwater debacle, "In your heart you know he's right," even if destined to overwhelming defeat; and the refusal of the Mississippi Freedom Democrats to accept LBJ's two-seat compromise. The movement is greater than the party; compromise risks the loss of all integrity, all authenticity.

David Horowitz, Peter Collier, and Ron Radosh represent "the God that failed" phenomenon, a second generation of disillusion and ideological flip-flop from left to right. Horowitz and Collier consider their own and the New Left's complicity in Black Panther crimes, especially the murder of a bookkeeper they provided to the party, to be the moment that forced them to come to grips with radical evil; in Radosh's case it was a combination of the trauma of being attacked by lefty friends over his critical examination of the Rosenberg case and a rejection of the left-wing romance with Third World revolutionary movements, especially in Cuba and then Nicaragua. Such "second-thoughts" conservatives seem more comparable to ideologues like Elliot Abrams and William Kristol—all still seemingly fighting old ideological battles, the sons as their fathers, vanquishing ghosts. They're grounded in counterattack and negativity, and they lack the mythic reservoirs, the popular passions, the affirmative visions of Webb, Noonan, Atwater, and, in some ways, Bennett. Their identity is established through their enemies.

My initial curiosity in the New Right baby boomers was stimulated by several sources. In his memoir *New York in the Fifties,* Dan Wakefield recalls that "from the end of McCarthy's power to the beginning of the Vietnam War protests, the last years of the fifties and the first few years of the sixties, young people of right and left lay down together like the lion and the lamb—sometimes more like the boy and the girl" (263).

Wakefield caroused at Greenwich Village's White Horse Tavern with the Clancy brothers, young Mike Harrington, bohemians from the *Voice,* and libertarians from Young Americans for Freedom. He was struck by the "unexpected new aggregration of young conservatives [who] began to form around Barry Goldwater at the 1960 Republican convention in Chicago," and by a 1962 Goldwater rally at Madison Square Garden that brought together eighteen thousand young conservatives. He assumed, as late as 1963, that campus conservatism was the wave of the future.

Wakefield suggests that "we lefty liberals and right-wing conservatives found more common ground of conversation and interest with one another than with all those people who didn't give a hoot about politics, the great yawning masses of the middle" (267). Here the two-ring circus of New Left and New Right activists is set, linked by their common revulsion for the corporate, suburban, bureaucratic realities they faced. They were rival youth movements, ill at ease with what seemed an end of ideology.

A second source leading me to the Sixties New Right was the Berkeley Free Speech Movement. The initial burst of campus activism, following the banning of on-campus fundraising by Friends of SNCC and the subsequent arrest and suspension of nonviolent resisters, involved what at that point was called the United Front of clubs, which in October 1964 demanded reinstatement and a defense of free speech and political activity. This front included not only Young Democrats, CORE, ACLU, Young Socialists of America (YSA), the Independent Socialist Club, SLATE (the campus political party), the W.E.B. DuBois Club, SDS, and Women for Peace, but also the Young Republicans and California Students for Goldwater. The initial burst of youthful activism was a rebellion against Middle American conformity; both SDSers and YAFers stood against the jocks and the Greeks who taunted them outside of Sproul Hall. The "newness" of both New Left and New Right was in their resistance to bigness, to impersonal, bureaucratic structures—big corporations, big unions, multiversities. The corporate liberalism attacked by the New Left intellectuals of *Studies on the Left* was analogous to the welfare state excoriated by the Austrian school of free-market economics. And, of course, a number of young conservative intellectuals like Garry Wills and Karl Hess, uncomfortable with the New Right's militarism in the Vietnam era, with its apologetics for corporate America, and with its racism, discovered that they could only pursue their principles by moving left.

I don't wish to exaggerate the similarities between the two ideological movements of the 1960s. Both contained contradictory mixes of elitism and populism, libertarianism and communitarianism. Both had a certain contempt for suburban life and for the older generation. Both had romanticized agencies of change—whether Third World oppressed or bold entrepreneurs. Neither understood that what most peasants, workers, and bourgeois want is less than heroic. Both generational elites pushed the culture toward aspects of liberation; the generational mass, that "silent majority" of baby boomers plus the rest of America, struggled to incorporate what was most useful to their lives and, like Humpty Dumpty, tried—and still try—to put the pieces shattered by both New Left and New Right back together again.

In Dan Quayle's much discussed *Murphy Brown* comments before California's Commonwealth Club, he identified himself as a baby boomer. First off, he claimed generational credit for the civil rights accomplishments of the 1960s. It is important to distinguish between ex-liberal and neoconservative figures like Bennett who supported civil rights and those who, in rallying for Goldwater, Wallace, and the Ronald Reagan of the 1960s and 1970s, opposed all such progress. There's no evidence, for example, that Quayle, whose family newspapers were staunchly Jim Crow, stood with the former. In the speech, he continues,

> I was born in 1947, so I'm considered one of those "baby boomers" we keep reading about. But let's look at one unfortunate legacy of the boomer generation. When we were young, it was fashionable to declare war against traditional values. Indulgence and self-gratification seemed to have no consequences. Many of our generation glamorized casual sex and drug use, evaded responsibility and trashed authority.

He goes on to suggest that, whereas most middle-class boomers returned to more mainstream values as they developed family responsibilities and careers, the poor did not. Thus, to Quayle, poverty rests on the "poverty of values" spawned by the Sixties generation.

Marilyn Quayle sharpened this generational attack during the Republican convention in Houston, declaring, "Not everyone demonstrated, dropped out, took drugs, joined in the sexual revolution or dodged the draft."

Two points. First, Marilyn Quayle lumps together behaviors that need to be disaggregated. Those who demonstrated didn't drop out; and opposing the draft doesn't seem to have any necessary linkage with drugs or sex. She is simply engaging in Sixties bashing. Second, while there certainly are aspects of the Sixties subject to criticism, the dilemma of the New Right is that much of what is now (à la Dan Quayle's comments on civil rights) approaching mainstream acceptance was the New Left agenda: equality before the law and inclusion of all historically aggrieved groups—African Americans, Latinos, Native Americans, women, the disabled, seniors, gays; opposition to a senseless slaughter in Indochina; sensitivity to environmental and health issues. All that is presently considered mainstream and much that remains controversial or "politically correct," as it moves toward the commonsense wisdom, comes from the New Left. And much that is problematical, particularly an erosion of community, a resistance to our essential interdependence, is shared by the Sixties movements, both of which celebrated versions of liberty at the expense of the whole. The New Left counted on either left-wing or pastoral utopias to contain "doing your own thing." The New Right, always more the party of memory than the party of hope, either relied on a Reaganite nostalgic past or simply walked away from the dilemma in its worship of the marketplace. Finally, the invisible hand of conservatives exerts as little restraint on the antinomian spirit as did passing joints or nonmaterial incentives.

The Sixties generation of new rightists has had considerable success in shaping the metaphors and therefore the politics of the past twenty-five years. David Keene, who went from New Right boomer to chair of the American Conservative Union, recalls:

> By 1968 and 1969, those of us who were active in the conservative movement knew for a fact that the ultimate result of what was going on was going to be just that, whether it was going to be Nixon or Reagan was a question, but we knew that these people who were out there rioting in the streets were handing us the country and for that we have something to be grateful for. (*Sense of the Sixties,* part 6)

As the Edsalls persuasively argue, the reactions to the Sixties rebellions generated the Reagan revolution of the 1980s. And much of that revolution was carried and implemented by traditionalist boomers like Dick Cheney, Vietnam vets like Jim Webb, thirties-cum-sixties ideologues like Elliot

Abrams and Bill Kristol, converts like Stockman, Horowitz, and Collier—but, I would suggest, most of all by those like Peggy Noonan, Lee Atwater, and Bill Bennett. They were touched by much of the iconoclasm of the decade, its essentially rock 'n' roll spirit, its fierce demand for liberty, its sense of humor, its antiestablishment, anti-elite sensibility, and, yes, its idealism.

Atwater, the least idealistic of the lot, sees TV as critical to the formation of his generation. He includes the unprecedented educational opportunities rooted in middle-class lifestyles, the integration of women into both higher education and the work force, greater leisure, and Vietnam. What Atwater calls "a new traditionalism," a new synthesis, rests on self-actualization, opportunity, a sense of quality, tolerance (the big tent indeed), a social conscience (which of course still indulges in Willie Horton ads!), gender equality, and an opposition to bigness. Sounding like the Port Huron Statement, Atwater concludes that possibly the greatest quality of boomer consciousness is a sense "of something missing in their lives." He doesn't stay long with this theme of alienation, instead, characteristically, exploring how Republicans can unify the libertarian baby boomers with the more populist, social-issue conservatives.

In fact, that is what the Republican Party wasn't able to accomplish in the 1992 elections and what it still struggles with since its 1994 success. The two Pats—Buchanan and Robertson—stand *against* the Sixties, in fact, against modernity. Atwater understood the need to create a new synthesis. After all, the movements of the Sixties—New Left, hippie, feminist, green, gay—have made fundamental demands on all of our lives. That there has been resistance should hardly surprise us. If we've learned anything from human history it should be that we are characterologically conservative creatures, slow to change. And we've been asked to change—from our most essential and intimate values about men and women, whites and blacks, straights and gays, to all of the things that affect our everyday lives. Who honestly doesn't resent separating garbage? Who doesn't sometimes curse seat belts? Don't many of us resent the self-righteousness of the bans on smoking? This latter point brings me to closure; the New Right's strengths have rested on the New Left's weaknesses—its self-righteousness, in fact, its elitism, its contempt for the lives of those who can't so easily bring behavior and values into line with reason and truth. This is the legitimate core of what has mostly been a demagogic attack on political correctness. In my own studies, this is the largest group within the Sixties generation, its silent majority. It has been a contradictory group, resentful of radical challenges, attracted to Nixon and then Reagan for patronizing their middle-class suburban virtues and aspirations. But its members *have* been changed by the Sixties, sometimes unwillingly, more often at their own pace, in their own good time. They are more tolerant in matters of race, gender, and religion, and premarital sex; they are more environmentally conscious. But they are also tougher on crime, more in favor of the death penalty and of their right to own weapons. And they are more suspicious of both government and business. In this sense, those who speak of a distinct generation—a Vietnam generation "touched with fire," or a "wounded generation"—are expressing a truth.

Newt Gingrich, born in 1943, a pre–baby boomer, is still inconceivable without the Sixties. His much discussed admiration for the Tofflers, his flash and dash of futurism, of high-tech sci-fi patter are part of the effort by Republican conservatives to be no longer merely the party of memory but simultaneously—and without so much as a blink—the party of hope. It is for these reasons that Gingrich calls himself a revolutionary; that so many of his congressional supporters do so without the slightest hint of embarrassment is a measure of how much the 1960s has shaped the New Right.

Gingrich's evocation of Franklin Roosevelt is a lesson learned from the master, Ronald Reagan; his cultural tolerances, especially his rhetorical affirmation of the integrationist civil rights revolution, mark his recognition of the need to bolster the conservative narrative of liberal betrayal.

There are twenty years between Gingrich and the Christian Coalition's executive director, Ralph Reed. Reed, born in 1961 in the latter years of the baby boom, leads the coalition's drive to broaden its programs, to soften its hard edge, to blend moral authoritarianism with economic libertarianism, indeed, to use a stealth campaign to achieve power.

Both Gingrich and Reed are shameless opportunists who nevertheless derive their power from movements of true believers—those evangelicals and fundamentalists who were politically energized by the cultural shock waves of the Sixties (climaxed by *Roe v. Wade* and those libertarian free marketeers), inspired by Hayek and Milton Friedman, and convinced that Keynes and Marx, and any proponents of a federal governmental role outside of domestic and national security, are an enemy whose time has passed. Their strength is from the seventy-three frosh congresspeople of the class of '94; from baby-boomer ethnics like House Budget Committee chair John Kasich (R-Ohio), whose family background, like that of Peggy Noonan, was straight New Deal Democrat; from straight-arrow libertarians like baby-boomer Vin Weber, who worked with Gingrich in establishing the Conservative

Opportunity Society in 1983. It is also from those dittoheads who resonate to Rush Limbaugh's blending of Paul Harvey and Wolfman Jack.

But, at the same time, we should recognize the destructive aspects of what Russell Baker characterizes as "segregation by calendar," a division both empirically and ethically dubious. Our baby-boom president, Bill Clinton, had greater support, for example, from those both younger and older than the Sixties generation. And matters of social class, race, and gender shape political behavior far more powerfully than does generational identity.

My own view is that the long-term impact of the movements of the 1960s rests on whether any activist group finds the way to help the mainstream—baby boom and otherwise—resolve the questions and challenges raised during the 1960s and still at the very heart of determining the survival of our culture and our nation. Most of our labels—generational, ideological—seem only to get in our way as we continue to redefine and reinvent our America.

Yuppie: A Contemporary American Key Word

Yuppie is one of the central key words of our culture. Precisely because of its contradictory, even confused meanings, it is part of a critical conversation taking place over the past two decades about, among other things, the meaning and legacy of the Sixties (another key word), the nature of the American Dream, the nature of work and its relation to reward, the system of social class and status in America, and the present conservative climate.

The term entered our consciousness well after the 1960s when *Newsweek* proclaimed 1984 "the Year of the Yuppie." The catalyst seems to have been pollster Pat Caddell's generational strategy for Gary Hart's presidential campaign, which highlighted the existence—and exaggerated the centrality—of a block of young, upwardly mobile professionals. Although the initial impetus for this categorization was electoral politics, increasingly it became associated with patterns of consumption and life-style. And the road to understanding its significance is through the ways in which issues of life-style have permeated our political culture.

The notion of the yuppie has been absorbed into our everyday vocabulary. References to yuppies range from a *New York Times* op-ed piece blaming yuppies for the decline of dads and sons playing catch in the yard to editorial cartoons ridiculing yuppies for their October 1987 stock market losses. Indeed, one can scarcely make it through a week of moderate TV viewing without confronting a stereotypically defined yuppie in a sitcom or drama. What accounts for the emergence of this remarkable character type?

Axiom One: The Middle Class Cannot Win

The middle class is condemned for either being boorish and vulgar or for being "yuppified."

Granted we are in the midst of an embrace, albeit opportunistic, of the middle class. But this love affair, this competition between Republicans and Democrats, conservatives and liberals, to pitch goodies, especially tax cuts, to the middle class, needs to be integrated with the recent cultural history of the middle class.

I have always found curious the glaring contradiction between the pre-Sixties contempt for middle-class boorishness, vulgarity, and kitsch and the post-Sixties ridicule of that section of the middle class who moved toward a more European sensibility. Recall that the 1950s were filled with cultural critiques of the American middle class: Newton Minow's assault on the wasteland of TV, John Kenneth Galbraith's critique of an affluent society enamored of gas-guzzling, tail-finned cars, and innumerable attacks on the ticky-tacky nature of the developing suburban landscape. This critique, building on a tradition associated with Sinclair Lewis and H. L. Mencken, bemoaned the tastelessness of the "booboisie"—ketchup on all meals, Rock Hudson/Doris Day movie tastes. Our best and most recent examples of such criticism are Paul Fussell's wickedly satiric *Class* and *Bad.* Indeed, a variety of powerful and diverse traditions—romantic, bohemian, conservative, Marxist—have anchored their laments concerning modern life in the spiritual poverty of the American middle class.

And what was the preferred alternative for such a varied lot of critics? Before the 1960s, most talked of European cinema (not movies), a more nutritious and delicate cuisine, less ostentatious (and less stuffed) furnishings—you can fill in the rest. It's what I would call a Europeanizing of the tastes of the American middle class.

Here is a fairly typical description of yuppies: "They travel widely, eat out often and shop for fine furniture and art . . . natural fabrics—no polyester, thank you . . . insatiable appetites for designer clothes, computers, video recorders, pasta makers, phone-answering devices, espresso machines . . . Volvos and BMWs . . . [yet] fashionable doesn't mean a high price . . . [for example] wood and natural fiber goods." Other than the implied critique of yuppies' insatiable desires, the description typifies much of what 1950s critics dreamed of instilling in middle-class behaviors—in short, good taste.

Am I wrong? Are the particular tastes of those called yuppies worthy of contempt? Certainly we can puff up our chests—we guys at least—and blow smoke about meat and potatoes, beer that isn't lite, real men don't eat quiche, but the fact of the matter is that most yuppie tastes are exactly what critics have always bemoaned as missing from American culture. Consider the improvements in American movies, from Scorsese to Tarantino, or restaurants since the 1950s as two cases in point.

So I am left with my first axiom of the concept of the yuppie: It reflects a no-win situation for the American middle class, held in contempt if boorish, equally subject to ridicule if cultured. No-win situations suggest a need to examine underlying, ambivalent attitudes toward middle-class America.

Axiom Two: Yuppiedom Is a Consumer Paradise

The contempt for yuppies reflects a populist suspicion that many affluent middle-class people receive undeserved rewards for unproductive, parasitic labor.

It may be useful to segment the middle class into its constituent strata. Yuppies are upper-middle-class people, highly educated folks, professionals who prefer the stimulation of the city to the presumed blandness of suburbia. Personal income is a factor: Yuppies are defined as those earning at least $35,000 per family in "a professional or managerial occupation" (1986 dollars). But income does not seem to be the central differential. For example, suburban upper-middle-class college grads with more conventional (that is, plebeian) lifestyles aren't usually included. Suburbanites with stylish tastes, on the other hand, increasingly are. One study simply uses the U.S. Census Bureau category of "professional and technical" and defines "urban" as living in a place with a population of at least a hundred thousand. However one slices it, those labeled yuppies are in the most affluent stretches of the upper or professional middle class but are not included among the wealthy—or at least not in early usages, as we shall see.

Many recent analyses suggest an erosion of the middle class beginning in the 1970s—we have heard a great deal about the necessity of two-income households, the high costs of college, the decline of union-wage jobs, the increase in part-time and low-paying service work. Within this framework, criticisms of the "insatiable" tastes of affluent yuppies make, at the least, demagogic sense. Hardworking Middle Americans resent the material trough available to the Sixties-generation people portrayed in TV series like *thirtysomething* or popular films like *The Big Chill*. So some part of yuppie bashing is rooted in such resentments, easily parlayed by politicians seeking populism without risk. Instead of addressing the more politically charged issues of widening income and wealth gaps, of the erosion of middle-class existence, PAC-funded candidates can ridicule the life-styles of the upper-middle-class sophisticates.

They can build on resentments against yuppies resentments to attack what conservatives call the new class or the political class, a variant of yuppie, a cultural elite defending the National Endowment for the Humanities, the National Endowment for the Arts, public radio and television, or the Smithsonian's exhibit on the *Enola Gay*.

What are the underlying images that create and deepen such resentments and, clearly, envy? The initial yuppie portrait circa 1984 suggested a certain shallowness and hypocrisy. One part of this critique relates to the nature of work and variations in reward. Yuppies aren't involved in basic industry, smokestack or high-tech; they make money from money, manipulate markets for their own profit, and provide highly skilled and rewarded services central to a capitalist economy—in banking, investment, real estate, money management, advertising, marketing, communications, and law. Yuppies are portrayed as experts in the arts of money, imagery, or both. They epitomize our ambivalence about the postindustrial economy we have been entering in the latter part of the twentieth century; they embody the "cultural contradictions of capitalism" analyzed by Daniel Bell—work ethic uncomfortably intertwined with hedonistic consumption. Work hard, play hard.

I think that a major aspect of yuppie bashing is a very traditional populist suspicion toward those who make a lot of dough without providing a tangible product or easily understood service. Our national mythology embraces work that is commodity producing, like farming or manufacturing, or at least putatively useful, like retailing clothes or hardware. It's a leap of imagination, even faith, to see *value* in writing advertising copy or in doing the paperwork involved in the bond market. And yet such professionals seem to earn significantly more money than a skilled engineer, a chemist, or, more obviously, a steel worker.

So, there is an aspect of yuppie bashing that reflects contempt toward those who not only flaunt their goodies but who haven't really done anything to merit such a bonanza of consumption. How did they earn it? Notwithstanding the old Smith Barney commercial featuring John Houseman ("We make money the old-fashioned way. We earn it."), most of us don't really believe that Smith Barney or any other money manager earns such fortunes. Of course, there's an ambiguity here—those labeled yuppies seem to be more on the professional than on the corporate executive/management side of affluence. And major corporate figures don't seem to be subject to the same kind of ridicule as yuppies. It is most curious that, precisely when yuppie bashing arose, U.S. culture celebrated "the life-styles of the rich and famous" and turned self-serving autobiographies by Lee Iacocca and Donald Trump into best-sellers. Iacocca, I suspect, stands on the safer ground of basic industry. Trump's popularity, because of his more parasitic sources of wealth and because of his extravagant life-style, seems more subject to the fickleness of celebrity mongers.

We seem to separate yuppie sophisticates (think Woody Allen movies or *thirtysomething*) from equally affluent business people (think the vice president of one of your town's local banks) from the truly rich and powerful. Part of this is the hint of parasitism linked to yuppiedom; unlike "real" businesspeople in the "real" world, yuppies don't seem to contribute anything as they manipulate money or words, two thoroughly untrustworthy symbolic activities.

In addition, yuppies are presumed to be highly selfish and therefore somewhat morally suspect persons. They are the heart of Tom Wolfe's "me generation"—self-indulgent in their consumer tastes and, more damagingly, in their personal lives. Think of Newt Gingrich's demagogic linking of Woody Allen with the Democratic Party's approach to family values. Yuppies seek self-fulfillment; they place self over others, especially family. They rationalize self-indulgence with "quality time" for their children, designer gifts, and child care. Many films and TV shows feature scenes of yuppies forced to choose between self and family. Yuppies are cosmopolitan, bereft of loyalties to community, but also lacking in the older, cosmopolitan virtue of intellectual and artistic passion. They merely consume books and paintings; their only passions are making and then spending money. As the saying goes, they seem to have life-styles but no lives.

I cannot for the life of me figure out why yuppies are more contemptible than other kinds of businesspeople, from middle managers to corporate bigwigs. What accounts for the special ridicule to which yuppies are subjected? Certainly, living in or near cities isn't more contemptible than living in plush suburbs; clearly, driving a BMW or Volvo isn't more immoral than having a limo or a Lincoln Continental. Is it possible we actually believe that yuppies are less interested than Chamber of Commerce types in having friends and some kind of family life? Like many of our sterotyped prejudices, yuppie bashing includes a goodly quotient of projection—those of us who are middle class and are facing the contradictory tensions of modern life are all yuppies in certain ways. Many college-based middle-income jobs are socially and morally problematic: How many lawyers do we really need? All studies indicate how top-heavy our corporations are (certainly compared with those of Japan) in management and managerial salaries. How many lucrative positions rest on intrinsically useful goods and services? Blue-collar workers have always looked askance at the rewards of those who push pencils. Our discomfort with yuppies reflects our historical ambivalence toward middle-class work and its rewards, compounded by the particular circumstances of the late twentieth century.

Axiom Three: Yuppie Bashing Is Sixties Bashing

Yuppie-bashing is a kind of counterattack on the movements, events, and counterculture of the 1960s and carries the implication that such phenomena were destructive and, worse, faddish.

I have withheld consideration of generational issues until now. And yet these issues have been at the very core of discussions of yuppies. If we put it into a story—and many have—we would imagine a baby boomer who was in college during the 1960s, touched by war protest, civil rights, women's rights, environmental concerns, and the trinity of sex, drugs, and rock 'n' roll. This boomer believed, innocently, that he would remain young forever, in either a revolutionized or "greened" America, a Woodstock Nation of peace, love, and pleasure. But, of course, our generational traveler, part of whose illusion rested on monthly subsidies from all-too-bourgeois parents, "chilled out" during the Seventies, compromised, dropped back in, abandoning much of his social commitment, and began to become—a yuppie. So, as Jonathan Schell has noted, this hippie or yippie evolved—or degenerated—into the yuppie. This is another version of the old tale of the idealistic youth having to come to grips with the hard realities of the marketplace. And, alas, this youth suffered double contempt—first for the pathos of his Sixties dreams, second for the shallowness of his consumerist present.

Yuppie bashing, as a variant of Sixties bashing, is the attempt to portray the social movements associated with the 1960s as anything from nihilistic to foolish, but in any case now passé, merely nostalgic. It is in this sense that those presumed to be yuppies are distinguished from their fellow affluents in the corporate sectors—they once had utopian visions, once assaulted old-fashioned values and behaviors. Now they've merely shifted the focus of their selfishness from marijuana and LSD to cocaine, from sexual to consumer promiscuity. And they had the moolah to "do it!" and, after all, "if it feels good, it *is* good."

Until quite recently, the yuppie was presumed to be either an ex-radical or ex-liberal or, at least, a watered-down version of either. Thus the contemptuous rebukes, "You don't even have the courage of your old convictions," or "You've sold out." Of course the bulk of those affluent and college-educated folks never had such ideals in the first place. I'm fascinated by this moral fine tuning: Those who once had hopes for social justice are held in contempt; those who have always been self-interested and oblivious to those in pain are let off the hook.

Axiom Four: Yuppies Are the Right's "Other"

Yuppie bashing has been an important element in the successful conservative strategy of stigmatizing white, affluent liberals as contemptible hypocrites.

Linked to concepts of "radical chic" and "new class," yuppiedom signals the conservative message that affluence and a social conscience don't mix. I trace this phenomenon to several conservative ideological thrusts, successful image making. Perhaps the most powerful of such images originated with our most influential Tory writer, Tom Wolfe, whose concept of "radical chic" subverted the pretensions of affluent liberals, smearing them as hypocrites, reducing them to ridicule as fashionable trendies slumming with demagogic black militants, succumbing to being "mau-maued." The image of the Leonard Bernstein fund-raiser for the Black Panthers, high above Manhattan, a veritable plenum of the cultural elite, is at the heart of the conservative strategy to define liberalism as contemptible.

Within the social sciences, especially as they pertain to social welfare policies, neoconservative intellectuals like Irving Kristol constructed a pseudotheory of the "new class," essentially the communications and academic networks held responsible for the excesses of the welfare state of the 1960s—affirmative action, busing, indulgent welfare costs, permissiveness in education, softness on crime, and so on. Both Wolfe's "radical chic" and the neoconservatives' "new class" rest on the unstated premise that affluent people, educated people who support causes associated with those in need are presumptively self-interested—in power, influence, boondoggle jobs, grants—and therefore they are suspect, hypocritical. Real men not only don't eat quiche, they don't care about poverty or war or pollution. These essentially sexist concepts, which helped build the Reagan revolution and now fuel the Gingrich mandate, fit neatly with the generational story of "chilled" yuppies.

Consider the ways in which Bill and Hillary Clinton fit the conservative story of yuppie and Sixties bashing. Both are part of the cultural elite, the new class; they are attorneys. Both were Sixties activists. Much of the assault on Hillary Clinton rests on the insinuation that she is less than a loving, caring mother, that she is not Barbara Bush. She's pushy, ambitious, an emasculator. And she's morally compromised; she made a yuppie fortune from suspect investments. And who is she? Where is she rooted? Why does she change her hairstyle and her clothing style and her public persona so often? Bill Clinton embodies so much of the conservative imagery— draft dodger, vacillating opportunist, denying pot smoker; a man who shmoozes, who is glib, a master of communications skills. The deep anger directed at the Clintons by the Gingrich right wing and whipped up by their demagogic talk-show allies rests on the ways stereotypes of a yuppie power couple, morally compromised by the movements of the 1960s, revealed by moments of hypocrisy, attach themselves to our First Family. As Newt Gingrich exclaims, they are *not like us*, they are McGovernite hippies. What we are experiencing is the power of a conservative myth as it shatters the liberalism initially built by the New Deal, linked with the Democratic Party, and in crisis since the 1960s.

The old New Deal coalition, seen as a narrative, set common working people against the big-money plutocrats. The coalition included capitalists, particularly those of immigrant stock unable to break through the nativist prejudices of elite Wasp country clubs. The GOP was stuck with the image of being partial to the special interests of Wall Street and Main Street, lacking the common touch. Much of the Rooseveltian rhetoric was demagogy, but it was close enough to some aspects of social reality to sell—at least until the late 1960s. Since then, the Republicans, initially inspired by the simple verities of Barry Goldwater and the darker appeals of George Wallace, have inched toward constructing their own populist coalition. Nixon called it the "great silent majority"; Ronald Reagan and now Newt Gingrich have brought it to astounding electoral success.

It's a reversal of the New Deal model: The silent or moral majority, Newt Gingrich's "real" Americans, is made up of the producers, the hardworking family people—those who don't protest (except for the pro-lifers, of course). The alternative, according to the Republican story, is an alliance of parasites, upper-crust new-class intellectuals, George Will's political class, from Ralph Nader to Dan Rather, from Murphy Brown to Woody Allen, with underclass welfare loafers and rapists, mostly black or Latino, illegal immigrants, teen moms, and so forth. What Middle America produces, the Democratic Party liberals want to spend on the newly defined "special interests"—a wonderful projection to which only a satirist of Thorstein Veblen's skill and wit could do justice—the poor, women, gays, labor. Republicans, alas, support working people, "hard hats," but not organized labor or—horrors!—unions. They have a contract *with* America which is, in many ways, a contract *on* those Americans denied legitimacy.

Thus the yuppie serves as an instrument in the creation of conservative ideology and domination. How? By smearing liberal Democrats as the party of yuppies—who, in their immorality, have no sense of spending limits, who just don't get it, who, as Dan Quayle has argued with great success, don't recognize that Murphy Brown is not just a television character but a personification of yuppie selfishness. By suggesting, à la Tom Wolfe, that a social conscience usually masks self-interest, opportunism, guilt, trendiness, or some combination thereof; by suggesting that affluence inherently mandates conventional business values and legitimate self-interest (for instance, demands for lower taxes), conservatives have ingeniously diverted villainy from actual centers of power—the multinationals and Wall Street—to arenas of mere status and life-style, Yuppie Heaven.

Axiom Five: Yuppies Are the Target of Political Myths

The stereotype of yuppies as culturally tolerant and economically conservative is false.

First of all there are actually very few yuppies within the baby-boom generation, somewhere between 1.1 and 2.4 percent of their cohort group. Sociologist John Y. Hammond concluded, on the basis of extensive survey analysis, that this small but privileged group is "more liberal than the general population on issues of personal freedom," but "not particularly conservative on social welfare issues," which contradicts "big chill" assumptions. Delli Carpini and Sigelman, examining similar data, find "almost no evidence" for the stereotype of economically conservative, socially liberal yuppies.

I would like to suggest that the contradiction between the

survey data profile and popular imagery points to the conclusion that yuppiedom is a self-inflicted wound of the culturally ambivalent professional middle class. Let me set a scene to develop my point: The former antiwar activist, now an attorney who balances making a good living with commitments to good causes, struggles mightily with the purchase of (fill in the blank) a nice car, a new home, a top-of-the-line computer. At bottom, the conservative cultural assault on yuppies relies on a kind of puritanism, an ambivalence especially deep in those who have liberal-to-radical social consciences, which takes the form of an obsession with the ways in which consumer goods can corrupt. The guilt-inspired, self-deprecating utterance "I'm becoming a yuppie" translates as a sellout to consumerism, to selfishness, to callousness. I suggest that those left of center tune in to the ideological message underlying their torment and refuse to participate.

There certainly is a radical tradition that focuses on attaining moral purity, saving one's soul, resisting the temptations of pleasure. But for all its strengths, that essentially religious tradition must be distinguished from a more pragmatic politics that focuses on one's work, on accomplishments, on results.

The Marxist tradition also has its problems with affluence. However, a movement that holds in contempt what most of its potential constituents desire—the good life—is hardly likely to get anywhere, and deservedly so. The radical who self-flagellates over the purchase of a microwave oven is likely to have censorious feelings toward the consumer spending of those at the lower end of the middle class. Deep down, one finds a lack of generosity *toward oneself,* which justifies the same righteousness toward all others.

Radicals have always been hard on themselves, which is in part a virtue, a source of moral strength in the face of the seductions of conventionally defined success. I'm not at all suggesting that radicals or liberals should just not worry and be happy. Rather, I am pointing out the tendency toward a severe form of self-criticism that can be used to justify a moralistic, repressive response to others, especially those whom one needs to persuade. If one spurns such people's aspirations as unworthy and invests only in a romantically conceptualized population of the *truly* oppressed and exploited, then one has effectively abandoned any hope of building a broad, democratic movement in the United States.

I think a case can be made that there has been collusion between Left and Right, to the infinite advantage of the latter, in telling the story of the 1960s. The Left devalues the mainstream, for example: The family is inherently pathological; sexual and child abuse is rampant; pornography is rape; suburbs are sterile; suburbanites are racists; patriotism is indefensible; dead, white European males merit no respect; U.S. history is a saga of genocide. All partial truths, all significant falsehoods, all measuring alienation from the faith, the desires, the values of most Americans. The history of all peoples is contradictory, full of shame and pride, moral failures and astounding strides toward freedom. The Right airbrushes all those contradictions, patronizing desired constituents, playing to much of what is ugliest in our traditions. But, in isolating what's half empty and in all too often ignoring or denying what's half full, the Left plays right into the hands of the Gingriches and the Helmses. And one part of that collusion is over the legitimate aspirations of Americans to pursue happiness by making their lives more comfortable.

Axiom Six: "Die, Yuppie Scum!"

The concept of yuppie can be demagogically used by all parties because it avoids substance by highlighting life-style.

We're in the midst of a cultural war of position and imagery over who has the rights to yuppie bashing. In fact, the liberal counterattack is one of the more interesting aspects in the evolution of the yuppie. The conservative "radical chic" cum "new class" cum yuppie parasite is countered by the liberal alternative, which initially flowered during the stock market mini-crash of October 1987. Pundits seemed more than gleeful, at that moment, at the financial troubles of young, callous Wall Streeters. The scandals involving Ivan Boesky and Michael Millken, merchandised liberally by Oliver Stone and Michael Douglas in the film *Wall Street,* shifted yuppie definitions somewhat away from generational themes toward becoming amorphous synonyms for selfishness and greed. As such, the yuppie becomes any young affluent adult who is excessively materialistic and self-centered.

The liberal counterattack, "Die, Yuppie Scum!"—the best-selling button at the 1988 Democratic convention—has been part of an effort to reconstruct the New Deal coalition, the people (Democrats) versus the interests (Republicans). The Democrats have sought to identify yuppiedom with the self-ishness of the Reagan years, with tax cuts for the rich, capital gains, and the widening income gaps between the rich and everyone else. Social critics like Barbara Ehrenreich have framed the issue as one of a fearful middle class facing declining standards of living, increasingly buying at K-Mart, resenting the conspicuous consumption of those feasting at the Reaganite trough.

The Republicans won that 1988 battle, linking Michael Dukakis to Carter and McGovern and Jesse Jackson and proclaiming themselves the party of the producers. The Democrats have been challenging that claim, with some success in 1992, less in 1988 and 1994. They plant themselves with the variegated middle classes against preppies (like Bush) and yuppies (like Quayle).

As we approach the twenty-first century, both parties seek to be identified as the populist champions of the middle class. What we do not see is a coming to grips with the more fundamental anxieties that have made the concept of yuppie so pervasive in our culture.

What is the basis of our reward system, such that corporate raiders and stock market manipulators make oodles while teachers, auto workers, and child-care workers struggle to make ends meet? To what extent are we at a competitive disadvantage because of the excessive number of our best-educated people choosing lucrative but wasteful careers in law, finance, real estate, and marketing? What are the real factors making it so difficult for everyday folks to sustain family and community life, to live morally? Are yuppies and hippies and feminists and gays the culprits? Are McGovernites? Or should we be looking to the businesses whose sales require an advertising industry that essentially tells us to say yes to almost everything?

We need to get past the pseudopopulist tendency to blame all social evils on Wall Street or on the mass cultural preoccupation with status and life-style and come to grips with the ways in which antidemocratic, corporate power shapes and distorts our capacity to achieve self-determination. When Dan Quayle flails against lawyers one day and Murphy Brown the next, we need to shape a response that places excessive litigation and family dysfunction in the context of substantive issues of power and interest: Who can hire the most talented legal representation? Who pays the advertisers and funds the TV shows and movies that market sensationalism, exploit sex and gratuitous violence? When George Will endlessly attacks the political class, we need to just as endlessly force him to address the implications for democracy of an unrestrained business community.

The history of the yuppie is part of an American pseudopopulism that mistakes appearance for reality, life-styles for power. It resonates with ambivalence about affluence and with enormous envy and resentment. It rests on a puritanism that mistrusts cosmopolitan tastes. It presupposes a false dichotomy between affluence and social conscience. Most of all, it avoids the essential questions of a democratic polity: How can an economy, a polity, and a culture so dominated by money be harnessed to democratic aspirations, to the quest for liberty? Or, to update Huey Long, "Share the wealth—but enjoy it too!" Enough with the hair shirts!

Clinton, Vietnam, and the Sixties

On Memorial Day 1993, President Clinton spoke at the Wall before an audience that included a vocal minority of hecklers. To such critics, Clinton was insulting the memory of all who served; he was not only a draft dodger but a liar and a coward. Some turned their backs to him. Most of the crowd was more respectful, hearing the president reiterating Colin Powell's quoting of Lincoln—"With malice toward none; with charity for all"—calling for a binding up of the nation's wounds.

Later that same day in a small South Jersey town following its Memorial Day parade, the ceremonies included a color guard of veterans and several patriotic speeches. What was striking about the service was the invisibility of Vietnam. None of the color guard unit were Vietnam-era veterans; most were Korean or World War II vets. During perhaps forty-five minutes of speechifying, all of which was conventionally patriotic, there was only a single mention of the Vietnam War, and that was as a part of a series of the wars we had fought. The keynote speaker, a local Republican politician, talked about the ways in which the Battle of Iwo Jima still speaks to us; it was an eloquent, impressive history lesson. And yet, the speaker is a baby boomer. He did not serve in the military; he did not get sent to Vietnam. He is a right-of-center conservative, characteristically hawkish, anti-Communist, at least until the Berlin Wall came down.

I find the two stories paradigmatic of our continuing difficulties in, as Gerald Ford implored us to do almost twenty years ago, putting Vietnam behind us. We are stuck in the Sixties, and a considerable part of that remaining presentness rests on the war (the other aspects I will address later).

First, the efforts by Ford and others to get beyond Vietnam, the characteristic American tendency to view history, à la Henry Ford and Jay Gatsby, as irrelevant, has not worked. Second, the effort by others to transcend Vietnam, to depoliticize it, to establish one big tent within which antiwar activists, war vets, and mainstream patriots could heal the wounds, has had only partial success. The Vietnam Memorial, the Wall, is an extraordinary place; it comes the closest to transcending ideology by focusing on the particularity both of those who died and of those who see their own faces reflecting off the black marble. But Clinton's rough experience on Memorial Day suggests that there is only so far that such transcendence can take us.

Consider another story, that of Katherine Ann Power's attorney, Steven Black, a Vietnam pilot who staged a mock warcrimes trial for himself, in which Power served as *his* attorney. He sentenced himself to community service at the same time as he negotiated the terms of Power's surrender.

I believe that to begin to understand, not to speak of resolving, the pain and anger, the wounds still festering, we must reconfigure the involved parties. For much of the past decade, we have been stuck with an unfortunate dualism: those who served, increasingly admired as prols, blue-collar heroes, versus those who protested, increasingly criticized as self-serving, hypocritical elitists. From Jim Webb's novels to Jim Fallows's influential article on social class and the draft, from *Platoon* to *China Beach*, the dualism has often *been* the politics of the war in recent years. It has a conservative and a liberal bent; the former tends to believe that we could and should have defeated Communist tyranny; the latter argues that it was, simply, a waste of American lives. The only opponents of the war granted respect in both scenarios are GIs, like John Kerry, and those protesters willing to go to jail for their beliefs (recall Myra MacPherson's important study *Long Time Passing*).

As discussed in chapter 4, we need, however, to begin with, not two, but at least three groups—those who fought, those who protested, and those who did neither. My *Class of '66* provides a case study of such people, at least the males, mainstream baby boomers, most of whom supported the war, voted for Richard Nixon, but found respectable, middle-class ways (such as the National Guard and reserves) to avoid possible combat. This group makes my South Jersey story relevant; they are people who still tend to avoid the issue or, if more hawkish in their adulthood, to be more defensive about their own behaviors. Are they Dan Quayles? Not quite, that wouldn't be fair. Few are as flat-out rich; few have been as baldly hypocritical. The flak that Clinton receives is in part a diversion of resentment away from those silent-majority baby boomers who are uncomfortable with the legacy and, especially, with the survivors of the war.

In a similar sense, the airport scenarios of antiwar demonstrators spitting at returning vets allow us to avoid the ways in which mainstream people, and not only baby boomers, made Vietnam vets uncomfortable with their awkward silences. Instead of fixating on the noisemakers hissing the president, we need to pay attention to the silences of those who remain haunted by their own passivity and insensitivity.

In making sense of the responses to Clinton, we need to emphasize that there is a right-wing agenda, a Sixties-bashing strategy, spearheaded by Newt Gingrich, the Quayles, and folks like Bill Bennett. Marilyn Quayle excoriated Sixties activists at the GOP convention in Houston. She worked to reenforce another myth, that of the irresponsible, hedonistic Sixties radicals whose permissive behaviors ravage our culture. First of all, we need to make certain distinctions. Those who opposed the war fall into two camps: radicals who saw the war as a symptom of U.S. imperialism, and liberals who viewed it as a tragic error. Among those radicals, there are splits over approach, levels of militancy. It is important to admit that many of the radicals romanticized the Vietnamese Communists, as they tended to romanticize all Third World liberation movements. This led them to some serious moral failings, some callousness toward human suffering and injustice committed by the Third World "Davids" against the U.S. "Goliath." It's important for these self-criticisms to be part of the story; Susan Sontag was indeed right to suggest that the radical press ignored or downplayed or rationalized Communist violations of human rights. Those of us who opposed the war, particularly from a radical, anti-imperialist stance, need to face our own blindnesses.

What's most interesting about Clinton is that he was not part of that most radical, militant wing of the movement. He was a dove, an intern in Bill Fulbright's office, a "Clean for Gene," Simon-and-Garfunkel kind of guy; he probably never did inhale and certainly was aligned with those like Allard Lowenstein who sought to save the system by reforming it.

Those like Clinton who sought to make the system consistent with its own ideals in matters of opportunity, democratization, and human rights, who stood with Gene McCarthy and Bobby Kennedy and Martin Luther King, Jr., need to directly challenge the Sixties bashing by the Right. They not only have nothing to be embarrassed about; they have much to defend with pride.

The Quayles focus on partial truths. Yes, there was indulgence and permissiveness; yes, there was mindless rebellion against authority; yes, there was some moral laziness. But examine our world, how far we've come—an end to U.S. apartheid, an enlargement of rights to African Americans, Hispanics, Native Americans, the disabled, women, gays. Okay, I know, we've got a long way to go. But those of us who remember Jim Crow, the problem that has no name, the time before anyone would even consider the possibility of the rights of gays in the military must recognize the achievements generated by the Sixties. Almost every advance came out of the troublemakers, the agitators, the radicals of that era, as their ideas were absorbed by the middle—diluted, softened, but integrated. Every survey of opinion sustains this achievement. To counter the real Vietnam syndrome, to effectively address Sixties bashing, we must cherish our victories. My goodness, they're rare enough!

The New Right provides another segment of baby boomers, characteristically ignored by most observers. Indeed they came out of the Sixties stronger, for more of the long haul, than did the New Left. As E. J. Dionne and others note, there are some striking similarities between New Left and New Right—a critique of the welfare state as bureaucratic and deadening, a call for liberty and community, a focus on the individual. We must credit the New Right with raising important questions about the dangers of the state and with persisting in a valuing of the role of markets in sustaining both human choice and economic efficiencies.

On the other hand, the New Right has consistently resisted the transformations that have moved the United States toward diversity, toward tolerance. Their criticisms of affirmative action, of political correctness, while often astute, are undermined by their suspect track record. Of course, it is a mark against the heirs of the New Left that they have allowed First Amendment rights to be so hypocritically co-opted by conservatives.

Regarding Vietnam, the New Right, the conservative movement, also has much to confess. Its members ideologized a struggle with a particular history, insisting that Vietnam was merely an extension of Soviet or Chinese aggression. They played with martial rhetoric at the expense of untold lives. And, when it was crunch time, they did not stand up and be counted. No senior-level officers, no insiders who believed in invading the North, declaring war, calling up the reserves, nuking Hanoi, came forward and resigned their commissions. And many who played hawk in later events, like Dick Cheney and Bill Bennett and Newt Gingrich and Phil Gramm, somehow managed, like the South Jersey politician in my second story, to avoid service.

And yet there is a compelling conservative issue, one that makes those on the Left uncomfortable, and one that helps to shape the response to Bill Clinton. It's made most eloquently by Jim Webb, John Wheeler, and William Broyles:

What is worth dying for? What does it say about a nation if it is uncomfortable with sacrifice, whether one is discussing national service or tax increases? One can interpret this challenge as particularly masculine. And in some ways I believe the ultimate gift of modern feminism is precisely a centering on what's worth living for. But the issue remains troubling, and it's very nature seems to me to be part of what haunts Bill Clinton, who neither served nor took many risks as an activist, always, as his now famous letter states, maintaining his options. Clinton's difficulties over Bosnia rest to a considerable degree in the ways in which his waffling highlights unresolved questions raised in the Vietnam era.

In all of this discussion we are considering elite opinion and behavior. In many ways, the legacy of the Sixties and of the Vietnam War rests on the rivalry between New Left and New Right elites, each seeking to persuade the mainstream of its case. The New Left, antiwar side has been charged with elite privileges, most sharply by Fallows's piece on Harvards and prols at the Cambridge draft board. Unfortunately this truth about Vietnam, which Christian Appy appropriately calls a working-class war, seems to be walled off from its broader implications. It's as if Fallows and others discovered that this is a society with social class and racial privileges and then applied this knowledge only to the war. What is unusual, unique about the Sixties and Vietnam is that elite youth, in part, broke with their well-paved paths to success. Most elite youth did not become antiwar activists or even antiwar sideliners; they may have done some dope and grown longer hair, but they remained career oriented, often oblivious to the changes and challenges surrounding them, and used their social-class advantages either to get deferments or to get into guard or reserve units.

At the heart of this dispute is the legacy of Tom Wolfe's notion of radical chic, the notion that affluent people who have a social conscience are morally suspect. Wolfe's cutting prose has been a significant factor in the virtual disappearance of political liberalism. One must agree with Wolfe that a politics of guilt generates wonderful material for a social satirist, from Leonard Bernstein parties for Black Panthers to the political correctness of Antioch's dating rules. But such an essentially conservative and cynical posture, what one might also call the P. J. O'Rourke school of cultural criticism, lets the country clubs and corporate boardrooms off the hook. Most affluent people don't have bleeding hearts or generous wallets; they live in suburban cocoons, insulated from the squalor of American life. And most powerful people are merely economically correct. The Wolfean metaphor, which stretches to a fixation on yuppies and *Big Chill* boomers, shifts the political and ideological ground from a focus on economic to cultural privilege, from power to status, from lives to life-styles. Recall the assumption by voters, before the convention, that Clinton was part of the elite, based on his Rhodes scholarship, his Yale law degree. He still suffers from this conservative framing, which, at bottom, suggests that a new class of intelligentsia, yackers, are our cultural elite, remote from mainstream values and behaviors, including patriotism and a commitment to service. Under this cultural framing, the billionaire Ross Perot becomes a populist.

It remains essential to note the racial and gendered distortions of most considerations of Vietnam and the Sixties. The division into those who served, those who protested, and those who did neither is a gendered way of conceptualizing a generation. Hillary Clinton now enters the foreground. She personifies the transformation that the Quayles and such have condemned; of course, Marilyn Tucker Quayle, finally, shares a Sixties story more with Hillary Clinton than she does with her husband. And the Supreme Court decision on sexual harassment in the workplace, driven by two female justices and supported by the most conservative—Antonin Scalia and Clarence Thomas—suggests that the center has shifted to the left in terms of women's rights. We owe such shifts to those, like Hillary Clinton, who have been in the forefront since the 1960s. What was once radical becomes mainstream.

Clinton's detractors juxtapose Colin Powell, Vietnam vet, with the commander-in-chief, reenforcing the conventional view that the working class and minorities fought while the privileged protested and avoided service. Such an obvious truth should not be allowed to stigmatize those who sought to "bring our boys home," at least without paying attention to those who simply took a hike, cultivating their private gardens. A strong case can be made that those who protested saved lives, both American and Indochinese. That should be a source of pride to Bill Clinton.

The issue of the Indochinese must be addressed; finally, the least satisfactory aspect of the ways in which we attempt to integrate the war and the decade with which it is associated is the invisibility of "the other," those at some distance from our attention, those whose over three hundred thousand missing in action generate no protest, those whose post-traumatic stress syndrome veterans pay the heaviest of prices, those who have had to struggle to build a nation following thirty-five years of warfare, those denied their claim to visibility—and honor—at the Wall.

It must be said plainly and forcefully that it is obscene for Americans to smugly criticize the Vietnamese for their economic screwups without at the same time paying attention to the ways in which the war brutalized their society and ravaged their landscape. This is not to return to a romanticization of the heroic Vietnamese; we surely know enough about the evils of Communist dictatorship to resist that illusion. They, like all peoples, must be held accountable for their behavior. But so must we. In our obsession with the MIA/POW issue, our vengeful economic warfare upon the Vietnamese, our resistance to the restoration of relations until 1995, we are like Tom and Daisy Buchanan, going on with our lives oblivious to the destruction our thoughtlessness has wrought.

Perhaps Clinton's move toward diplomatic recognition, a courageous act even granted its support within the business community, will help us integrate the Indochina war into our historical record. Certainly he has been assisted in this regard by the support of Vietnam veterans like John Kerry, Bob Kerrey, and, especially, conservative Republican John McCain. But the responses to Clinton's move suggest that we haven't been able to get on with our lives, to get past Vietnam, to heal all of the wounds. There's still too much hurt out there. This is what Bill Clinton needs to find a way to address.

At his best, as a new kind of Democrat, he is able to understand the need to move beyond some of the worn-out rhetoric of both Right and Left, willing to see that we are in a new ball game with new challenges. I admired him, standing there at the Vietnam Memorial that Memorial Day, but I was uncomfortable with him almost physically hiding behind Generals Powell and Jesse Brown, with his defensive if empathetic words.

Why not stand proudly as an heir of the best of the Sixties, its refusal to reduce love of country to knee-jerk allegiance, its expansion of rights to all previously excluded groups? He can be proud of what his segment of a generation has wrought and, at the same time, be generous and ecumenical with those whose values have led them to other choices. He needs, as well, to continue to criticize the worst legacies of the Sixties, the righteousness and snobbery of the well educated.

For Bill Clinton to have any chance to win over many, never all, of his critics and to regain the respect of many of his former supporters, he needs to recognize that it's not enough to think about tomorrow; one must speak out on those traditions of the past that can help us get there. Sadly, he may be characterologically incapable of such consistency, as David Maraniss suggests in his biography; but, at the same time, we must be careful about too quickly assuming his demise. He can no longer play "the comeback kid"; that's become tiresome. Most of all, he needs to no longer communicate being merely a "kid," someone without the gravitas, the maturity, to lead this nation.

The Sixties: Legacy

It was the summer of 1968; I was watching the pre-
liminaries to the Democratic convention in Chicago. I
had no desire to be there. First of all, I didn't see what
impact we, that is, the antiwar movement, would have
on a convention sure as hell about to nominate the pa-
thetic Hubert Humphrey. In addition, I didn't like the
kinds of rhetoric spouted by radical and countercultural organizers. I was at best bemused, but mostly
annoyed, with the notion of a Yippie Festival, a spec-
tacle of nominating Pegasus the pig and mocking
the conventioneers. And the increasingly Marxist-
Leninist rhetoric of SDSers, the hackneyed language
and attraction to confrontation, the essentially thera-
peutic politics—"We need to escalate the tactics because we'll burst if we don't"—alienated my obnox-
iously practical bent.

It was as I had felt a few weeks earlier, at an Independence Day picnic at a friend's house. Some picnickers

had just returned from the hothouse excitement of the Columbia University building takeovers and bust. They were literally thrilled, high on the cameraderie, the sense of community, the glimpse of liberation. I kept asking, "But what
does it mean to 'liberate' Columbia? Can you hold it? What
would you do with it?" They resented my probes; so would I
in their position. They kept saying, "You don't understand. If
you were there, you would understand. We can't express
what we felt; it was extraordinary."

In fact, my first disaffection from New Left politics had
been the Pentagon March. The new confrontational style, the
essentially theatrical strategy, and the new countercultural
presence (for instance, levitating the Pentagon with collec-
tive vibes)—all left me cold. It was the first major antiwar
demonstration I did not attend.

So, during the summer of 1968, I was beginning to despair
of the movement that I had joined three years earlier with
great enthusiasm. I had spent part of the early summer visit-
ing a dear friend in California. Danny was a former SNCC organizer, now working for a progressive union. We were on
our way back to his brother's house, high on a Santa Cruz
mountain, bringing the beer to help us with a sumptuous
pasta dinner. We talked about the upcoming conventions
and the November election as we drove up into the hills. It
was a few weeks following the murder of Robert Kennedy. At
a certain moment, we both came to understand that Richard
Nixon would be our next president. It wasn't great insight,
merely a fuller awareness of something we, among others,
had kept at bay. Danny pulled the pickup truck over to the
side of the road. And we sat and stared. No words passed between us. Just the frustration and awe of what was before us.
After three years of antiwar effort and more in the civil rights

struggle, the country was going to elect Richard Milhous
Nixon president. It was profoundly depressing. Finally, Danny
started up the engine, and we returned to his brother's house.
The beer was getting warm.

Later that summer, I was sitting in my bedroom watching
the preconvention analysis, when the news flashed—"Soviet
tanks have entered Czechoslovakia." Prague Spring, the momentous effort by Communist Party reformers led by Alexander Dubcek to establish what they called "socialism with a human face," a truly democratic socialism, was crushed. I was
crushed. I angrily thought of all the left press editorials making light of rumors of Soviet troop movements. I was a Marxist intellectual. I believed that capitalism, however modified,
lacked the capacity to deliver on the promise of liberty, fraternity, and equality; that capitalism, even in its Politics-of-
Growth/welfare state mode, was at best a half-full democracy,
political but not economic. To me, socialism was political
democracy plus economic democracy; as I cribbed from a
friend, I was a socialist *because* I was a democrat. As such, I
thrilled to the Czech experiment, the beginnings of civil liberties, press freedom, free expression within a cooperative social order. I read everything I could find on worker activity,
intellectual and student ferment, profiles of leaders; and I saw
such pieces as part of a global effort, positioned in the United
States within the New Left, within SDS in particular, toward
participatory democracy, toward democratic socialism.

What struck me then and stays with me now, almost thirty
years later, was the obliviousness of *most* of my radical peers
to the Czech effort. They weren't typically hostile, except for
those already enamored of the harshest Stalinist models, who
saw Dubcek and Svoboda as revisionists. Rather, they were un-
caring. It didn't matter to them; it simply didn't touch them at

all. Why was that? Why did this promising effort to democratize Communism have no significance to most new leftists?

Stanley Moore, the British Marxist, provided part of the answer back then. He argued that Marx had two visions, one a politics of liberation, the other a sociology of change. The politics of liberation was Marx's utopian dream, communism, the end of prehistory, the postscarcity social formation within which the rule became "from each according to ability, to each according to need." This stage of communism was a vision of community, of the end to alienation, of the promise of Renaissance men and women fishing in the morning, writing poetry at noon, inventing and constructing according to human need rather than human greed before dinner, and so on.

On the other hand, what Moore called a sociology of change was rooted in the first stage, socialism, during which the law of value, and consequently the marketplace, still had weight. Under socialism, capitalist exploitation was eliminated, but inequalities based on contribution remained, that is, from each according to ability, to each according to contribution. Socialism, with its conflicts, scarcity, division of labor, was clearly less glamorous, less visionary. Moore argued that Marxists needed to abandon the politics of liberation as not only utopian but destructive. The dream of communism, in basing itself on unrealistic expectations of human behavior, drove idealists toward Rousseauist corruption, forcing people to be free, imposing on them when they did not fulfill the radical intellectual's expectations. In brief, the communist utopia always inherently risked the Stalinist nightmare of totalitarian dictatorship.

I found Moore's argument cogent; indeed, I found the possibilities of a mere socialist stage quite glamorous, thank you very much. But few of my political peers did. They were invested in Fidel and Che, in Cuba's quest to build the new socialist man, in Mao and the Chinese Cultural Revolution, in utopian dreams, communitarian desires. Czechoslovakia couldn't fulfill those longings; it was too sober, too practical, too Western, too familiar. American new leftists would travel to Prague and argue with Czech activists over the value of First Amendment freedoms. They were full of Herbert Marcuse's notion of repressive tolerance, that bourgeois democracy's seeming commitment to liberty was essentially a form of totalitarianism, a one-dimensional closed room only available to those with power. Czech youth couldn't understand this sophisticated argument. To them, being able to speak one's mind was wondrous; they knew what it was like not to have that right. They knew what it was like to face governmental repression if they spoke up. U.S. radicals rarely did.

So when the police engaged in what the Walker Commission appropriately labeled a police riot against the Democratic convention protesters in August, American youth turned toward the TV cameras and imitated their Czech counterparts, chanting "The whole world is watching!" What they didn't understand is that they were testing the hypocrisies of a functioning if flawed political democracy; the Czech rebels had been seeking to establish precisely those liberties so many new leftists viewed as secondary if not bogus.

Why do I introduce a concluding chapter with stories of Columbia, Prague, and Chicago? I want to use my own experiences to set a framework for what I hope are the beginnings of an examination of the significance of that tumultuous decade. One of the themes I have stressed throughout this book is that of the utopian overreach of the radical movements of the 1960s. Part of this overreach is consistent with a powerful set of currents within the American experience: an antinomian impulse often linked with an urge toward perfectionism. From the earliest moments in the history of this most Protestant of all cultures, there have been radical expressions of an extreme individualism, roots of "doing your own thing," and desires to overcome social tensions with a quest for the kingdom of God on earth. These distinctively Protestant conflicts between individual and community— being *in* society but not *of* it, organizing a priesthood of believers each committed to their conscience's dictates, and seeking a Christianized society through the conversion experiences of individuals—informed the 1960s movements, for example, the beloved community of SNCC, the participatory democracy of SDS.

The dystopia for Americans has never been George Orwell's *1984;* it has been Aldous Huxley's *Brave New World.* Only our obsession with the Cold War enabled the grayness of totalitarian group-think, the stark shabbiness of Winston Smith's world, to be perceived as an American possibility, although we have certainly heard sufficient newspeak to keep Orwell's vision relevant. Most cultural critics, however, resonate more with the ways in which freedom is corrupted, not by the fist or the iron heel, but by human pleasures, the fulfillment of human wishes, what Herbert Marcuse clumsily called repressive desublimation, the transformation of desire into an instrument of manipulation and domination. Both Left and Right shared such concerns, both feared the buying off of citizens through welfare state largesse, the conversion of citizens into mere consumers.

The cultural war we have been engaged in since at least the 1920s is more three- than two-way. There are the most sophisticated folks, the "cosmopolitans"—urbane, educated beyond college at the more prestigious institutions, living in professional, upper-middle-class, often called yuppie enclaves like Marin County, Westchester County, university towns, bucolic pockets in Vermont, Maine, Oregon. At the opposite end are the "provincials," those most insulated from, and most resistant to, the challenges of modernity, of cultural relativism. Many such folks inhabit the small towns and most insular suburbs, belong to the most evangelical or fundamentalist churches. They have been fighting a rearguard action at least since the Scopes trial. Finally, there are those in between, the "locals," defenders of a Middle American individualism, most characteristically living in the suburbs, more uprooted than the provincials but more engaged with family networks than the cosmopolitans. They embody what pollster Daniel Yankelovich described as "the weak form of the self-fulfillment search" more strongly felt by cosmopolitans. They have been more open to cultural challenges concerning racial and sexual equality, lately to appeals for fairness regarding gays; they mistrust government, but as much in regards to issues of censorship as to issues of taxation. In brief, they tend toward a libertarianism that exists in tension with their longings for family and community and their nostalgia for a politics that might successfully articulate a notion of the public interest.

That notion of a public interest collapsed as a consequence of the battles, Left and Right, associated with the 1960s. What Robert M. Collins calls "growth liberalism," the Politics of Growth, could not be sustained under the stresses and strains of economic crises compounded by challenges to political legitimacy. The liberal consensus described by Godfrey Hodgson in *America in Our Time* had serious limitations, but it did usher in what economists call the golden age of U.S.

capitalism; indeed, it spearheaded a Western, increasingly global set of advances that seemed to permanently legitimate the mixed economy of the welfare state.

The left movements of the 1960s, inspired by the challenges the civil rights movement made to that liberal consensus, built by an affluent, highly educated segment of a generation, focused on those left out of the consensus—African Americans and other minorities at home and Third World peoples abroad; they raised serious questions about the character of a democracy limited to occasional votes for candidates too often beholden to powerful, moneyed interests; they questioned the definitions of success and fulfillment in a corporate economy consumed with profit making; and they expressed concerns about the recklessness with which great powers seemed to be willing to risk global annihilation. Conservative rebels during the Sixties shared with their left-wing peers concerns about the decline of community, albeit finding more to blame in government bureaucratization than in corporate villainy.

Most of the popular and academic work examining the 1960s is single-mindedly generational. There is an assumption that the Sixties translates as a generational moment, one exclusively for what new leftists called the Movement. Virtually none of the attempts to make sense of the 1960s see conservative challenges as more than reactive to the more radical movements. None of the flood of histories and anthologies of recent years devotes even a chapter to right-wing movements among baby boomers. Few give more than passing consideration to those baby boomers who were and remain the audience for both New Left– and New Right–inspired visions and programs.

Most of the efforts by Movement veterans—Todd Gitlin,

Tom Hayden, Mary King, Wini Breines—share this appropriation of the decade. Within this dominant if problematic framework, the arguments tend to focus on what went wrong, when it went wrong, and why it went wrong. One approach, most associated with Gitlin, posits a "good" Sixties associated with early SDS; the Port Huron Statement; the heroic period of civil rights activism through, perhaps, Selma; and the early opposition to the Vietnam War. It sees problems arising in the middle to late 1960s as the movement turned in contradictory ways toward a more guilt-driven politics of confrontation, Marxist-Leninist dogmatism, and countercultural indulgence.

As we have moved from memoir to monograph, from activist recollection to scholarly reconstruction, historians such as David Farber tend to align with Gitlin, suggesting that the period is a tragic story with "no simple legacy," in which racial and gender hierarchies were "subverted—but not overthrown," liberty expanded but our "moral compass" lost. Farber is least sympathetic to those with the most utopian politics, including those within the New Left and the counterculture contemptuous of everyday Americans: "The New Left and the protesters simply never spoke about work as a locus of political consciousness or radical energies. . . . No one seemed to pay attention to the hard work, the daily grind, to the effort it had taken so many Americans to make something from nothing" (295). Here is where some of the lines seem to be drawn. A variety of former activists and contemporary scholars, including Edward P. Morgan and Stewart Burns, seem more invested in the utopian, liberatory aspects of the 1960s, even as they note its excesses. Barbara Ehrenreich, for example, takes her stand with what she claims are the most radical qualities of the New Left:

The student Left rejected a vision of socialism as essentially a redistribution of what there is to have within capitalism. They did not want "more," they wanted something qualitatively different. . . . If there was a rupture on the left in the 1960s, it was because the New Left at its best had less in common with the socialist tradition of the Second, Third and Fourth Internationals than with the utopian socialism of the nineteenth century, with anarchism, and with situationism. (234)

Ehrenreich wants "to resurrect the alternative vision of human liberation, . . . not only economic justice, but also radical democracy and participation" (234). One finds similar sentiments in Morgan, Burns, Barbara Tischler, and Sohnya Sayres, Anders Stephanson, Stanley Aronowitz, and Frederic Jameson, the coeditors of *The Sixties without Apologies.*

The intraprogressive arguments are increasingly nuanced but often rest on attitudes about the human capacity to fulfill liberatory visions. Figures like Gitlin and Farber are more wary of what they see as the self-destructive and self-deceptive aspects of all forms of utopian thinking; they have joined liberal and social-democratic voices in developing a new respect for the limits of human plasticity. Radicals like Breines remain deeply critical of capitalist compromises and hold to what they see as a prefigurative politics with transformative possibilities.

The more sobered observers certainly make their case concerning the self-destructive thrust of the Movement as it engaged in a thoroughgoing rejection of all but its most visionary projects. But the more visionary critics are on firm ground in seeing more continuity in the trajectories of movement activism. The early New Left, as James Miller suggests, was caught between a civic republicanism and an existential search for authenticity, between a demand that the liberal welfare state live up to its own ideals and a vision of a participatory democracy that went well beyond Lyndon Johnson's Great Society, between a critique of Cold War demonology and a romantic attraction to Third World revolutionary communities, between changing the world and changing themselves.

In the process of struggling with these tensions, the early Movement suffered from its youthful isolation, compounded by its tendency to eschew all advice from Old Left and liberal voices. Its antinomian and perfectionist spirit made it difficult to establish the kinds of institutional structures, including those concerning leadership, that might have helped it weather the fire storms of an imperial war, the explosion of ghetto riots, and the rise of a youth counterculture. It was caught up in what became a near-global movement that, in the last days of the golden age of capitalism, viewed liberalism as the essential enemy.

My own reading, as much of the foregoing might suggest, leads me to lean toward the antiutopian analyses of Gitlin and Farber. David Stiegerwald, whose book *The Sixties and the End of Modern America* is certainly among the most thought provoking, argues that too many Sixties radicals, in their quest for a transformative politics, engaged in a

> silencing of a large part of the population which was not racist, that lived the inequalities of U.S. society, that was not particularly keen to embrace consumer culture, and that struggled to hold on to values in disrepute—independence, hard work, patriotism, and pride among them. The unrepresented in the sixties were that oft-mocked repository of decency, common Americans, white, black, Hispanic, Appalachian, and otherwise, who held to the work ethic, saw through the liberal hypocrisy and militant boasts, wanted simply to be given room to live. (242)

Peter Levy's work cautions us about the stereotypical conflicts assumed between radical youth and blue-collar prols during the 1960s; he points to the many instances of alliance and coalition between the Movement and organized labor. However, it seems to me that a fair case can be made that the ideological movements of the 1960s—New Left but also New Right—paid precious little attention to the life experiences of most nonelite working people, despite all protests to the contrary. The New Left, in particular, was oblivious to the ways in which cultural contradictions were stretching the ability of Middle Americans to sustain family, community, and work.

Barbara Tischler is certainly right to call for, indeed to anticipate, more case studies of 1960s movements and events not limited to the most highly publicized, elite locales. Such case studies will give us an increasingly complex and contradictory picture more fitting to such a cacophonous decade. Scholars such as Tom Bates, W. J. Rorabaugh, Tony Edmonds, Marc Jason Gilbert, and Kenneth J. Heinemann have begun the exploration of particular college campuses.

The Sixties rests on a dual and contradictory critique of the dominant projects and ideologies of midcentury: modernization theory, the mixed economy, the welfare state, corporate liberalism, countervailing powers, the vital center, the end of ideology. From the very outset, young new leftists both challenged the liberal center to fulfill its promise to complete the work of the welfare state (that is, to establish comprehensive, universal security for all Americans) and to address qualitatively more radical issues associated with notions like participatory democracy, authenticity, the beloved community. The best the welfare state could accomplish, à la Scandinavia, was a society in which there were rich, mostly middle-class and working-class people, and no poor. Youthful conservatives, indeed, feared the likelihood of such an accomplishment, aware that it would make it that much more difficult for them to persuade their fellow citizens that such accomplishments came at the cost of their liberties, were indeed the road to serfdom.

The accomplishments of the Sixties—more accurately of the always uncomfortable but finally necessary alliance of radical activists and liberal politicians, the yin and yang of progressive reform throughout the century—are remarkable. We moved from legal apartheid to an inclusion of African-Americans into full citizenship. And in the process, we came to address a host of issues of human rights and political empowerment. It was not simply the passage of the Civil Rights and Voting Rights Acts; it was the coming to grips with all non-Anglo-Saxon, Wasp voices; if black was beautiful, all colors, all ethnic identities were also lovely. It is true that such a welcoming occurred precisely as a homogenization of the consumer culture was taking quantum leaps, indeed, global leaps; but nevertheless the promise of a transnational America, of the kind of cultural pluralism and toleration advocated by Horace Kallen and Randolph Bourne, came closer to fulfillment. Legitimacy was extended to racial minorities, Catholics and Jews of Eastern and Southern European stock. And challenges arose from Native Americans, Asian Americans. And women. And gays and lesbians. And the developmentally disabled.

We have had some difficulty integrating these challenges into what was once a Wasp, male monopoly. It's striking in the film *Apollo 13* how white and male NASA was in 1970; today's flights are a measure of how far we have come. It would be hard to underestimate the extraordinary nature of this accomplishment, particularly as ethnic hatreds rage in many parts of the world. There is a fundamental notion of fairness within the American creed; all, not just men, are created equal, all merit equal opportunity. The postwar period struggled to hold back some of this progress, already in motion during the New Deal and clearly inspired by the struggle during World War II against Nazism.

The problems we face have to do with how difficult it is to recognize sameness and difference simultaneously. Alan Wolfe argues that both identity politics and Gingrichism, the heirs of Sixties New Left and New Right movements, are uncomfortable with paradox. He suggests that paradox is most central to liberalism because it opens the door to what is contradictory, ornery in both everyday life and politics. Paradox is at the heart of the compromises James Madison wrought in the creation of our constitutional system; paradox is what drove the poignancy of Lincoln as he sought a Union with "malice toward none"; paradox is the aristocratic FDR leading—sometimes being led by—the populist New Deal. Things are more than singular; they are multiple, complex, contradictory. We are many things as well as one thing.

It is interesting that what has come to be called identity politics began at a moment the doors opened to diverse voices, at the point at which Wasp domination was broken or at least forced to pay attention.

Part of the answer is that the cultural doors opened precisely as the economic ones seemed to be jamming. Tremendous pressures confronted the U.S. economy, pressures to provide access to previously marginalized groups, at a time when the golden age of U.S. capitalism was slowing down. In fact, it's remarkable, as economist Frank Levy demonstrates, how much the economy accommodated working women and blacks during a period of stagflation. Indeed, without the additional income provided by working moms, the emerging income inequality we have experienced since the early 1970s would be that much worse.

Such economic woes, which certainly are one way to mark the end of the Sixties, carry weight, but at least as important is that by the late 1960s, the movements of the Left had turned away from liberal ameliorative reforms and embraced a fully utopian set of visions, a contradictory mix of utopian socialism, romance with Third World revolutionary movements, flirtation with a cultural revolution centered on sexual liberation, psychedelia, and rock 'n' roll hedonism. As such, there was no way for even the most reformed liberal consensus to satisfy radical desires for community, authenticity, and individual expression.

Godfrey Hodgson labels his chapter on the hippie counterculture "Telegraph Avenue, Son of Madison Avenue." The counterculture did contribute to a very much needed loosening up of a buttoned-down, crew-cut, and sexually hypocritical culture. Daniel Bell's cultural contradictions were reaching a breaking point during the conformist Fifties; the liberatory explosion was all the greater for being suppressed for so many decades. An economy of mass production required mass consumption, and that necessitated a comfort with human pleasure.

The movements of the Left remained ambivalent about this development. Their romantic premises led them to believe that nature, perhaps assisted by electrified music and chemistry, would reconcile with culture and economy, that the desire for pleasure could not be harnessed or manipulated by corporate America; or that the countryside of the world would conquer the imperial cities. Most of all, their contempt for those living in "little boxes made of ticky-tacky" in working- and middle-class suburban America, precluded them from understanding the contradictoriness of this new pleasure-driven, consumer culture. When the counterculture crashed, when Woodstock Nation devolved to Altamont, when the horrors of Maoism were revealed, from Cambodia's killing fields to Tienanmen Square, when Sixties-based revolutionary projects collapsed for all but Alexander Cockburn and other true believers—all that remained was a postmodern sensibility that tended to reduce all universal claims to matters of power: at best, a loyalty to one's identity group; at worst, a smart-ass hipness best exemplified by the cynicism of David Letterman.

Identity politics rests on the flip side of that cynicism, a utopian set of expectations and demands that cannot be met—by definition—within any version of the prevailing social order or any realizable alternative. For this reason, the extraordinary successes of the movements that spawned identity politics must be characterized by its ideologues as insignificant or co-optive. And without a realistic vision of the good society, without a notion of the public interest—indeed, with a suspicion that all such notions are instruments of domination—aggrieved groups tend to be merely, exclusively victims. That there are victims is undoubted; but a sense of victimhood does not lead us toward a pluralist democracy—it is limited to appeals, grievances, guilt trips, reparations, public displays, rage, and vengeance.

And yet, those movements upon which identity politics rests at their best once moved mountains. They helped to make us a fairer nation—racially, ethnically, sexually, environmentally. But the tone by the early 1970s, on the Left, was apocalyptic. The revolution had failed—or at least was derailed for as far as the eye could see. Nixon's great silent majority was in the saddle; reaction ruled. Or did it?

One of the problems in establishing the periodization of the Sixties is that so much happened in the first half of the 1970s. The second wave of feminism, gay liberation, and environmentalism only begin to become significant movements in the late 1960s. Many of the legislative accomplishments often associated with the Sixties actually were passed and implemented well into the Nixon years: for example, the Freedom of Information Act, the Environmental Protection Act (EPA) and the Occupational Health and Safety Act (OSHA) passed in 1970; significant increases in Social Security and in the food stamp program occurred in 1972; Supplementary Security Insurance (SSI) was passed in 1972; and the important Rehabilitation Act, which extended antidiscrimination protection to the physically disabled, was enacted in 1973.

The U.S. military efforts in Indochina didn't end until 1973, nor our military and economic involvements until Saigon fell in the spring of 1975. Of course, to many observers, the Watergate scandal that drove Nixon out of the White House in 1974 marked the end of the decade.

The successes of Nixon's electoral strategy, built on George Wallace's right-wing populism and the Sunbelt conservatism initially inspired by Goldwater, were in many ways reactions to the radical movements of the 1960s. A silent majority was being called upon to quiet, in fact, to crush, a noisy minority of radicals, hippies, militants. But that noisy minority had already succeeded in transforming the political landscape, both in the persuasiveness of its claims to make the U.S. system more consistent with its professed ideals and in the righteousness of its demands as it sought to overturn the system root and branch.

The system could barely address the more adaptable of the Movement's demands, and certainly not its most visionary ones, given the strains within the polity and the culture. The citizenry's central nervous system was frayed, at loose ends, and in need of relief. The Sixties radical movements were demanding not only that the system live up to its rhetoric; they were simultaneously calling for the replacement of the system. The slogan "No justice, no peace" arrived just as most Middle Americans were in need of a time-out, a break from the multiple demands placed on them in matters of race, gender, morality, behavior, identity.

The group perhaps most in touch with this exhaustion was the influential intelligentsia usually called neoconservatives. The neoconservatives were, in fact, the postwar, Cold War liberals who had constructed the ideological supports for the welfare state. They had embraced Arthur Schlesinger, Jr.'s "vital center," neither laissez-faire conservatives nor statist Marxists. Their most important contribution to the culture was their sobered post-Marxism, their awareness in the context of Hiroshima and Auschwitz that life is essentially tragic; that, in the spirit of Freud, we are obliged to make life less unhappy; that the discontents of civilization are nothing as compared with the destructive forces always within the hearts of humankind.

This vital center, best represented by Hannah Arendt and Lionel Trilling, by Irving Howe and Daniel Bell, by Reinhold Niebuhr and Richard Hofstadter, by writers like Saul Bellow and Bernard Malamud, offered the possibility of a maturing of U.S. political culture, a Europeanization. It was not a representative group, these mostly New York intellectuals— Jewish, urban, male. Trilling wrote of the absence of a genuine American conservatism; yet one can make a strong case that these thinkers were the embryo of a conservatism, a tradition based on U.S. ideals of democracy, liberty, and opportunity but tempered by concerns about mass society, totalitarianism, other direction, organization men, faces in the crowd, the paranoid style, anti-intellectualism. They were liberals aware of the social realities of evil—of Hitler and Stalin and Joe McCarthy.

This Depression generation of formerly radical, now liberal, indeed increasingly conservative intellectuals was unprepared for the challenges of the 1960s. For one, they too often had violated their own sense of human limitation in their commitments to Cold War policies, at least until Vietnam became a slaughterhouse. In brief, their anti-Communism sometimes got the best of them, leading them toward the very absolutisms they characteristically criticized. And they were unprepared for the vehemence of the charges directed against them by the New Left upstarts. The New York intellectuals were situated to be the teachers and guides to a younger, more affluent, more American generation of academic intellectuals. They carried the lessons of the Thirties, of Stalinism, of appeasement, of socialist realism, of a sentimental liberalism and a manipulative radicalism, of inappropriate foreign models.

But their warnings, their cautionary notes, their wisdom were scorned by most new leftists, who longed for commitment, for authenticity, for transcendence, for everything the soon-to-be neoconservatives saw as dangerous to both self and society. They all too often responded to their youthful critics with haughtiness and impatience; they were too quick to see a reckless adventurism or, worse, totalitarianism in the New Left's actions. There was a generational conflict, as Lewis Feuer argued in the heat of battle, but it was at least as much the fathers getting angry at their ungrateful children as vise versa.

One consequence of the 1960s was the rise of these neo-conservatives, whose prominence within the academy, the mass media, and the high culture insured them of a prominent voice. Indeed, as many of their critics argue, they, not their enemies, most fit the profile of a "new class." But their value, as part of the legacy of the Sixties, has been in their initial call for a more sober welfare state tempered by "the limits of reform," by "the law of unintended consequences," by the kinds of paradoxes Alan Wolfe sees as essential to a functioning liberalism. Neoconservatives understood the ways in which the radical challenges concerning race, gender, values, nation, and nature were unsettling to hardworking Middle Americans.

Unfortunately, too often their more polemical voices, like Ben Wattenberg's, took the counteroffensive in charging the Sixties movements with being un-American naysayers, out of touch with that housewife in Dayton, Ohio. Some of them, like Samuel Huntington, feared "an excess of democracy" as the consequence of Sixties demands for empowerment.

The tragedy of neoconservatives is that they became too embittered by what they called the new politics, that of the McGovernites, and increasingly locked in to dogmatic positions on foreign policy. As their focus became more ferociously anti-Communist, they tended to align with the more conventionally conservative Republicans building around the candidacy of Ronald Reagan. In addition, their domestic concerns about identity politics, especially affirmative action, busing, multiculturalism, Afrocentrism, radical feminism—their fundamental concerns about traditional values and behavior—drove them toward the Reaganite New Right. Sadly, by the early 1980s, the neoconservatives had for all practical purposes thrown in their lot with the uncomfortable conservative mix of free-market economics and moral authoritarianism. What held them together were common enemies—primarily international Communism, but, after 1989, mostly what can only be called Sixties bashing.

The New Right conservatives took advantage of the opportunities offered by a faltering liberalism unable to find win-win solutions to a stagnating economy in a new era of global competiveness and under pressure from a variety of constituencies with contradictory agendas, none of which established or even anticipated the public interest. The New Right simplified the initially more sophisticated neoconservative critique of Sixties utopianism and rode Sixties bashing toward the new conservative ascendancy. The conservatives invented wedge issues, instructed initially by the right-wing populist Kevin Phillips and his Sunbelt strategy, then by the frat-boy shrewdness of Lee Atwater: they played the race card, asserted their cultural solidarity with Middle Americans, waved the flag on all occasions, and stood up for what many still believed, despite all evidence to the contrary, was the American family.

It's a wonder that they did so well, given the enormous changes wrought by the Sixties. William G. Mayer and his associates at the University of Michigan have examined changes in public opinion from 1960 through the late 1980s. They write of "the whole recasting of American views about race, gender, and sexual mores," a radical transformation: toward greater tolerance concerning racial equality and opportunity; fundamental changes concerning the role and status of women, including egalitarian views of the family and of women and work, and an acceptance of sex outside of marriage; strong support of environmental protection. Such changes across generational lines would suggest a continuing leftward movement. So what explains the tendency toward the Right?

For one, these trend lines include more conservative shifts as well. Most important is the greater support for law and order. Support for the death penalty has soared, for example, as has support for longer sentences, skepticism about rehabilitative approaches to penology, and opposition to gun control. Conservatives have made great gains in harvesting the holders of such punitive views.

Such repressive responses are essentially opportunistic; they reflect cynical manipulations of fearful citizens. Since the 1960s, our prison population has quadrupled; we now house more prisoners per capita than any comparable industrial nation. No one suggests that we are any safer.

Where conservatives *have* contributed to the legacy of the 1960s is in their tenacious commitment to the value of the free market in maximizing human choice. During the golden age of U.S. capitalism, when it seemed that, as JFK noted, economic problems had been reduced to the merely technical because of the success of Keynesian techniques of fiscal and monetary interventions, the conservative devotion to the free market seemed quaint and irrelevant. It wasn't that liberals denied the market, but rather that they saw public authority and planning as the most efficient means of harnessing economic power and achieving economic goals; they assumed that an inexorable trend toward the welfare state defined modernization.

Conservatives deserve credit for reminding all of us—especially liberals and socialists—that the market has sensitivities rarely demonstrated by public authority, that whether one remains within a capitalist or moves toward a socialist economic structure, there will always and ever be an essential need to respond to consumer demand.

What we are seeing as we approach the end of the twentieth century is an ideological glorification of the free market quite analogous to that which liberals and Marxists once ascribed to central planning. Experience in Eastern Europe suggests that such ideological zeal is as foolish and counterproductive on the Right as it once was on the Left. If we are fortunate, all parties will come to understand that all effective economies require some mix—this can vary enormously—of market and planning, private and public authority. But the legacy of the Sixties is not particularly helpful in this regard.

I believe there is value in attempting to frame the various ideological challenges mounted to the welfare state during and since the 1960s. Too often interpretations restrict themselves to the left movements and examine conservative critiques only as reactive to the period's radicalism. There certainly is some truth in such a view, but it tends to simplify the complex and contradictory voices of the period. We need to affirm how important the more radical challenges were and remain: it is impossible to overestimate how much the civil rights, feminist, and environmental movements have transformed the political culture. Even the Gingrich Congress, as reactionary and mean-spirited as it is, is informed—and therefore limited—by those transformations. Conservative efforts to take us back in fact presuppose most of what were once the radical axioms of racial and gender equality and the need to protect the environment. Hypocrisy is indeed the tribute vice pays to virtue. And those on the Left do themselves and their constituents no service in exaggerating the reactionary threats; they are real enough.

The critical group often ignored in the literature on the

1960s are those baby boomers who neither fought nor protested, who didn't flock to Woodstock, that great silent majority of a generation to whom the Sixties carries less resonance. That such people now tend to vote more conservatively than other generations must be duly noted; that such baby boomers also have been fundamentally affected, over time, behind their backs, by the racial, gender, and environmental movements may prove more decisive.

Throughout these chapters, I have suggested that a central weakness of the left-wing and sometimes liberal approaches has been their discomfort with the suburban working and middle classes and the lives they have chosen to lead. The utopianism within the New Left and its successors in identity political movements has been deeply intolerant, even contemptuous, of the struggles of mainstream Americans to sustain family life and make a living in an increasingly fragmented and insecure environment.

A model of the Sixties must include both the libertarian and the traditionalist challenges made by those inspired by William F. Buckley's *National Review* fusionism and by the Goldwater electoral movement. They shared with those on the left a mistrust of concentrated power, at least in the public sector, and a fear that modernization was subverting those face-to-face primary institutions upon which civic culture rests. That they were oblivious to the threats posed by corporate power; that they were willing to sacrifice essential liberties, risk nuclear war, and associate with a variety of international thugs to engage in an anti-Communist crusade; that they were on the wrong side of the struggles to face up to our racist past must be weighed against their important if dogged insistence that the market mechanism is an essential institution to any democratic society.

Historians of the Sixties need to pay greater attention to the challenges posed by the neoconservatives, to the ways in which they express the tensions within postwar liberalism, to the possibilities that they express as the embryo of a genuine American conservatism, and to the tragic loss that their surrender to Reaganism suggests.

Daniel Bell, whose notion of "the cultural contradictions of capitalism" informs much of this book, once described himself as economically a socialist, politically a liberal, and culturally a conservative. That's too mechanical a formula, especially in attempting to address the cultural transformations—from dress to language to sexual behavior—associated with the Sixties. Peter Clecak comes closer to a helpful model when he argues for a reconciliation of traditions, a recognition that we desperately need the ballast of a traditional, Burkean conservatism with its respect for the weight of history, to temper the liberatory thrust of liberalism and the egalitarian zeal of socialism.

There was a smugness to the notion of an end to ideology as there has more recently been with the idea that we are at an end of history. Perhaps a little humility is due from all sides, all of whom carry terrible burdens of moral obtuseness, all of whom can make legitimate claims to advancing humankind, none of whom have demonstrated any ability to anticipate a variety of earth-shattering developments.

When my students submit the oral histories of baby boomers I require of them, it is interesting to see what their respondents remember about the Sixties. All mention where they were when Kennedy was shot, most discuss the missile crisis. One of the interesting dividers has been the space program, highlighted by the Apollo moon landing in 1969. Those who don't mention it are typically those more caught up in the cultural rebellions of the times. But to many of those interviewed, Neil Armstrong landing on the moon is one of the highlights of their youth. Few of the present examinations of the 1960s discuss in any depth or even mention in passing this remarkable effort. Why is that?

Even though there is an aspect of the counterculture that was literally driven by the image of the earth as seen from the moon—"the whole earth," Spaceship Earth becoming metaphors for environmental fragility, for the realities of human interdependence and the consequent need for harmony and tolerance—the predominant response of Sixties radicals to the space program was either hostile or oblivious. Many political activists tended to argue that money was being wasted in space that was needed here on earth to address issues of poverty; in addition, since the space program was so much a vehicle to beat the Soviets in the race to the moon— to be first on the moon—it was easy to reduce NASA to a Cold War instrument. Finally, many cultural rebels, as romantics, were suspicious of technological rationality; they valued the spiritual, the irrational, the non-Western, and so on. What more embodied Western civilization's promethean drives to dominate nature than the Apollo program?

Interestingly, Norman Mailer stood apart from this tendency within the Sixties movements to scorn the space program. His *Of a Fire on the Moon* was a thoughtful if narcissistic account of his own ambivalence and then admiration for the Apollo 11 effort. He was "Aquarius" in the year of Woodstock; the astronauts were "the knights of the silent majority." That's a wonderful metaphor for this other aspect of the Sixties, celebrated by those outside the Movement, living for the most part in the very same kinds of suburbs the Apollo astronauts inhabited. It may also be useful to note how this program, presently in eclipse, stands as a measure of the ability of the federal government to achieve great things.

The Sixties left many legacies; one of its most problematic has been the declining faith in the possibilities of government, particularly the federal government. All surveys indicate a declining willingness to invest any confidence in the capacity of government, in the domain of politics, among all Americans, but especially among baby boomers. Those of the Sixties generation seem to be more tolerant on cultural matters, less tolerant on crime, and more cynical about politics and politicians. Both New Left and New Right have contributed to this phenomenon; both trashed the role of government in constructing a welfare state. That one saw government as doing too little, the other as doing too much is less significant than that both contributed to the assault on liberalism.

And yet that erosion is not reducible to such assaults. For one, many of the New Left, neoconservative, and conservative criticisms needed to be made. Liberalism had become smug and self-satisfied; it did promise more than it meant to deliver, for example, the War on Poverty; it often was arrogant, bureaucratic, corrupt; it suffered from what William Leuchtenburg had criticized in New Deal liberals:

> They retreated from conceptions like "tragedy," "sin," "God," often had small patience with the force of tradition and showed little understanding of what moved men to seek meanings outside of political experience . . . the liberals, in their desire to free themselves from the tyranny of precedent and in their ardor for social achievement, sometimes walked the precipice of superficiality and philistinism. (342)

And, most critically, they had avoided a number of key issues through adaption of the Politics of Growth. So that when the golden age of U.S. capitalism began to reach its limits, liberals lacked the intellectual and ethical responses to face the challenges posed by its radical and conservative critics. They were in a quandary when choices had to be made, when there had to be winners and losers—a zero-sum game. Liberalism suffered a crisis of confidence, and such remains its plight. The much noted malaise that Jimmy Carter ascribed to the American people, in fact, was more true of political liberalism. And conservatives were there to take full advantage.

The New Left movements succeeded in transforming the culture and polity but failed abysmally in becoming a credible, institutional force. It's an old story that they self-destructed. More noteworthy is that they opted for their most utopian visions precisely as the U.S. and world economies were forcing downward readjustments in the parameters of the possible. It's striking to examine the ways in which radical feminism inhabited an ideological environment defined by Third World Maoism, gender essentialism, and Dionysian sexuality, precisely as the changing economy was more and more requiring two-income households to sustain middle-, even working-class, standards of living. The black power movement, in opting for a Third World solidarity more symbolic than substantive, looking backward to African glories and forward to Fanonian retribution, tended to overlook, except in the most rhetorical manner, a present in which its urban communities were being ravaged by deindustrialization.

Eric Hobsbawm's *Age of Extremes* reminds us of the ways in which the Sixties is only a part, a significant part, of what he calls the "Short Twentieth Century," from the Great War through the collapse of the Soviet system. He reminds us that the golden age was a Western, even a global phenonemon and that it followed what he calls the Age of Catastrophe that included two world wars, Nazism, the Holocaust, Stalin, the Great Depression. Indeed the 1960s New Left–based movements were part of a global set of eruptions, from Berkeley to Tokyo.

We must therefore understand that the American Sixties was part of an international youth-based movement that challenged mostly Western welfare state structures and that those structures, seemingly stable and robust, encountered strains that still define the last years of the twentieth century. In all cases, the New Left movements self-destructed, but inspired a variety of remarkably transformative processes addressing how we define race, gender, nation, nature, morality, and humanity. One legacy of the 1960s is how we have been struggling to sustain and extend these processes in a moment of economic crisis. It explains why it's been so difficult to make sense of the Sixties; it would be difficult enough for a society to absorb and integrate fundamental challenges to finding unity in diversity, to reconfigure how men and women relate to one another and the consequences this has for children, to figure out how to sustain prosperity without doing in the planet on which we temporarily reside, to come to grips with the ways in which we can allow more pleasure into our lives without destroying the basic values upon which our civilization has rested, to absorb a culture of abundance that nevertheless rests on scarcity, and, finally, to make lives for ourselves, rather than life-styles—this would be difficult enough to accomplish in a quarter of a century, less than two generations, if economic growth remained the norm. But all of these stresses and strains on the system have been compounded by the stresses and strains of a flat, problematic economy.

That economy has become global. The relative obliviousness of the New Left–based movements to the space program is similar to its willed ignorance about the scientific and technological advances, most strikingly computerization, that have transformed the globe over the last twenty-five years. Instead of fighting Vietnamese Communists, we now, finally, seduce them with entry to a world of powerbooks and fiber optics; there are no dominoes falling, or hard rains either— thank goodness; only our respective ideological pants as recent history has moved in directions no ideologies anticipated.

The legacy and meaning of the Sixties remain to be written. This book attempts to give some inital shape to that effort. We each write our own story and hope that it resonates with an audience sharing our perverse desire to make sense of our own lives. In my case, I begin with the New Left and New Left– inspired movements, most particularly the civil rights, feminist, and environmental movements. All raised essential challenges to our then prevailing liberalism. And all left indelible imprints on our democracy, enriching it, extending and deepening its roots and its flowering. But all tended to forget that life doesn't move in straight lines. And all suffered from the consequences of their respective impatience. They too quickly turned on those meant to be participants in their participatory democracy; they too often came to hate those not willing to embrace their beloved community. And the resisters, the silent majority of working- and middle-class people, turned to more complimentary if sometimes disingenuous voices.

The legacy of the 1960s includes the continuing decline of trade unionism, now at its lowest ebb since the early 1930s, and the related depression on salaries and wages of working people. The voices of the Right, the Rush Limbaughs and John Kasiches, have had success making populist claims, mostly by playing to Middle American resentments. But progressives have made their job easier; despite an obvious demagogy, there is indeed something accurately called political correctness. Our students smell it a mile away and smirk when we mouth the untenable.

Since the Left began to rhetorically shout "Power to the People," an ugly mindless gesture most demeaning in its glaring contempt for most of that very group, it has had difficulty in convincing Middle Americans that it has their interests at heart. In fact, it often has not. It has presumed the worst—the most racist, the most sexist, the most homophobic, the most philistine, the most fascistic—in those who remain central to any project with democratic aspirations.

There has already been all too much Sixties bashing and Sixties apologia. Perhaps it's time to examine this remarkable decade in all of its contradictoriness, valuing its enormous contributions, recognizing the problems it intensified, and placing it within a framework of time and space that continues to see the project of this short twentieth century as the fulfillment of democratic promise. The most extraordinary accomplishments of recent years, most particularly the liberation of Eastern Europe from Soviet domination and the triumph of Nelson Mandela and the African National Congress in destroying apartheid in South Africa, find their inspiration in the best that the Sixties movements offered, the notion of overcoming someday all forms of tyranny and providing all citizens with the promise of both liberty and democracy. On the other hand, utopian visions and identity politics seem to inexorably yield nightmares, righteous murders, xenophobia, ethnic cleansing. They invariably require myth in place of truth, rationalization in the face of unpleasant facts, forms of correctness when life's contradictions kick you in the ass. The legacy of the Sixties should remind us that good intentions aren't enough.

Bibliography

Alterman, Eric. "Elliot Abrams: The Teflon Assistant Secretary." *Washington Monthly,* May 1987.

Anderson, Terry H. *The Movement and the Sixties.* New York: Oxford University Press, 1995.

Appiah, Kwame Anthony. *In My Father's House.* New York: Oxford University Press, 1992.

Appy, Christian. *Working-Class War: American Combat Soldiers and Vietnam.* Chapel Hill: University of North Carolina Press, 1993.

Asante, Molefi Kete. *The Afrocentric Idea.* Philadelphia: Temple University Press, 1987.

Atlantic County Department of Regional Planning and Development. "Atlantic County Census Trends, 1970–1980." May 1985.

Babbitt, Bruce. "The Bully Pulpit: The Two Faces of Bill Bennett." *Washington Monthly,* July/August 1988.

Baskir, Lawrence M., and William A. Strauss. *Chance and Circumstance: The Draft, the War, and the Vietnam Generation.* New York: Vintage, 1978.

Bates, Tom. *Rads, A True Story of the Sixties: The 1970s Bombing of the Army Math Research Building at the University of Wisconsin and Its Aftermath.* New York: HarperCollins, 1992.

Bell, Daniel. *The Cultural Contradictions of Capitalism.* New York: Basic, 1976.

————. *The End of Ideology.* New York: Free Press, 1962.

Bell, Derrick. *Faces at the Bottom of the Well: The Permanence of Racism.* New York: Basic Books, 1992.

Bennett, William J. *The De-Valuing of America.* New York: Summit, 1992.

Berman, Marshall. *All That Is Solid Melts into the Air: The Experience of Modernity.* Magnolia, Mass.: Peter Smith, 1977.

Beschloss, Michael R. *The Crisis Years: Kennedy and Khrushchev, 1960–1963.* New York: HarperCollins, 1991.

————. *Mayday: Eisenhower, Khrushchev, and the U-2 Affair.* New York: Harper, 1986.

Boaz, David, ed. *Left, Right, and Babyboom: America's New Politics.* Washington, D.C.: Cato Institute, 1986.

Bowen, Ezra. "Preacher, Teacher, Gad-fly: A Profile of William J. Bennett." *Time,* July 18, 1988.

Branch, Taylor. *Parting the Waters.* New York: Simon & Schuster, 1988.

Braungart, Margaret M., and Richard G. Braungart. "The Life-Course of Left- and Right-Wing Activist Leaders from the 1960s." *Political Psychology* 11 (1990).

Breines, Wini. *Community and Organization in the New Left, 1962–1968: The Great Refusal.* New Brunswick, N.J.: Rutgers University Press, 1989.

————. "Whose New Left?" *Journal of American History* 75 (September 1988): 528–545.

Brennan, Mary C. *Turning Right in the Sixties.* Chapel Hill: The University of North Carolina Press, 1995.

Brown, Elaine. *A Taste of Power: A Black Woman's Story.* New York: Pantheon, 1992.

Broyles, William. *Brothers in Arms*. New York: Knopf, 1986.

Bunzel, John H., ed. *Political Passages: Journeys of Change through Two Decades, 1968–1988*. New York: Free Press, 1988.

Burns, Stewart. *Social Movements of the 1960s: Searching for Democracy*. Boston: Twayne, 1990.

Cagin, Seth, and Philip Dray. *We Are Not Afraid: The Story of Goodman, Schwerner, and Chaney and the Civil Rights Campaign in Mississippi*. New York: Bantam, 1991.

California Newsreel. *Berkeley in the Sixties*. 1991. Videocassette.

Carmichael, Stokely, and Charles V. Hamilton. *Black Power: The Politics of Liberation in America*. New York: Vintage, 1967.

Carson, Clayborne. *In Struggle: SNCC and the Black Awakening of the 1960s*. Cambridge: Harvard University Press, 1981.

Carter, Stephen L. *Reflections of an Affirmative Action Baby*. New York: Basic, 1991.

Caute, David. *The Year of the Barricades: A Journey through 1968*. New York: Harper & Row, 1968.

Chafe, William H. *Never Stop Running: Allard Lowenstein and the Struggle to Save American Liberalism*. New York: Basic, 1993.

———. *The Unfinished Journey: America Since World War II*. New York: Oxford University Press, 1986.

Clecak, Peter. *Crooked Paths: Reflections on Socialism, Conservatism, and the Welfare State*. New York: Harper, 1977.

———. *Radical Paradoxes: Dilemmas of the American Left, 1945–1970*. New York: Harper & Row, 1973.

Collier, Peter. *Destructive Generation*. New York: Summit, 1990.

Collier, Peter, and David Horowitz. *Second Thoughts: Former Radicals Look Back at the Sixties*. Lanham, Md.: Madison, 1991.

Comer, James P. *Maggie's American Dream*. New York: New American Library, 1988.

Cose, Ellis. *The Rage of a Privileged Class*. New York: Harper, 1993.

Crawford, Alan. *Thunder on the Right*. New York: Pantheon, 1980.

Crouch, Stanley. *Notes of a Hanging Judge*. New York: Oxford University Press, 1990.

Cushman, James. "James Webb's 'Fields of Fire.'" *New York Times Magazine,* February 28, 1988.

Daly, Mary. *Gyn/Ecology.* Boston: Beacon, 1979.

Davis, Flora. *Moving the Mountain: The Women's Movement in America Since 1960.* New York: Simon & Schuster, 1991.

Delli Carpini, Michael, and Lee Sigelman. "Do Yuppies Matter?" *Public Opinion Quarterly,* 1986.

Dickstein, Morris. *Gates of Eden.* New York: Basic, 1977.

Didion, Joan. *Slouching toward Bethlehem.* New York: Noonday, 1968.

Dionne, E. J. *Why Americans Hate Politics.* New York: Simon & Schuster, 1992.

Draper, Hal. *Berkeley: The New Student Revolt.* New York: Grove, 1965.

DuBois, W.E.B. *The Souls of Black Folk.* New York: Fawcett, 1961.

Duneier, Mitchell. *Slim's Table.* Chicago: University of Chicago Press, 1992.

Dworkin, Andrea. *Pornography: Men Possessing Women.* New York: Dutton, 1989.

Early, Gerald, ed. *Lure and Loathing.* New York: Penguin, 1994.

————. *Tuxedo Junction.* New York: Ecco, 1989.

Easterbrook, Gregg. "Here Comes the Sun." *New Yorker,* April 10, 1995: 38–43.

Echols, Alice. *Daring to Be Bad: Radical Feminism in America, 1967–1974.* Minneapolis: University of Minnesota Press, 1989.

Edmonds, Anthony O. "The Tet Offensive and Middletown: A Study in Contradiction." *Viet Nam Generation: The Big Book, Nobody Gets off This Bus,* Special Issue (1994): 119–122.

Edsall, Thomas Byrne, and Mary D. Edsall. *Chain Reaction: The Impact of Race, Rights, and Taxes on American Politics.* New York: Norton, 1991.

Ehrenreich, Barbara. *The Hearts of Men: American Dreams and the Flight from Commitment.* Garden City, N.Y.: Anchor, 1983.

Elshtain, Jean Bethke. *Democracy on Trial.* New York: Basic, 1995.

————. *Public Man, Private Woman.* Princeton: Princeton University Press, 1981.

————. *Women and War.* New York: Basic, 1987.

Evans, Sara. *Personal Politics: The Roots of Women's Liberation in the Civil Rights Movement and the New Left.* New York: Vintage, 1979.

Ewen, Stuart. *Captains of Consciousness.* New York: Pantheon, 1976.

Fallows, James. "What Did You Do in the Class War, Daddy?" *Washington Monthly,* October 1975.

Faludi, Susan. *Backlash: The Undeclared War against American Women.* New York: Crown, 1991.

Fanon, Frantz. *Black Skins, White Masks.* New York: Grove, 1967.

————. *The Wretched of the Earth.* New York: Grove, 1968.

Farber, David R. *The Age of Dreams: America in the 1960s.* New York: Hill & Wang, 1994.

————. *Chicago '68.* Chicago: University of Chicago Press, 1988.

————, ed. *The Sixties: From Memory to History.* Chapel Hill: University of North Carolina Press, 1994.

Feuer, Lewis. *The Conflict of Generations.* New York: Basic, 1969.

Firestone, Shulamith. *The Dialectics of Sex.* New York: Bantam, 1970.

Flacks, Richard. *Making History: The Radical Tradition in American Life.* New York: Columbia University Press, 1988.

Fox-Genovese, Elizabeth. *Feminism without Illusions.* Chapel Hill: University of North Carolina Press, 1991.

Foucault, Michel. *The Archeology of Knowledge.* New York: Pantheon, 1982.

————. *The Order of Things.* New York: Vintage, 1973.

Freedman, Samuel G. *Upon This Rock: The Miracles of a Black Church.* New York: Harper, 1994.

Freeman, Jo. *The Politics of Women's Liberation.* New York: David MacKay, 1975.

————, ed. *Social Movements of the Sixties and Seventies.* New York: Longman, 1983.

Friedan, Betty. *The Feminine Mystique.* New York: Dell, 1963.

Friedman, Thomas. "Clinton, Saluting Vietnam War Dead, Finds Old Wound Is Slow to Heal." *New York Times,* June 1, 1993.

Fussell, Paul. *The Great War and Modern Memory.* New York: Oxford University Press, 1979.

Gans, Herbert J. *Middle American Individualism: The Future of Liberal Democracy.* New York: Free Press, 1988.

Gates, Henry Louis, Jr. *Loose Canons.* New York: Oxford University Press, 1992.

Gilbert, James. *A Cycle of Outrage: America's Reaction to the Juvenile Deliquency in the 1950s.* New York: Oxford University Press, 1986.

Gilbert, Marc Jason. "Lock and Load High School: The Vietnam War Comes to a Los Angeles Secondary School." *Viet Nam Generation: The Big Book, Nobody Gets off This Bus,* Special Issue (1994): 109–118.

Gilligan, Carol. *In a Different Voice.* Cambridge: Harvard University Press, 1982.

Gitlin, Todd. *The Sixties: Years of Hope, Days of Rage.* New York: Bantam, 1987.

———. *The Twilight of Common Dreams.* New York: Macmillan, 1995.

Glazer, Nathan. *Affirmative Discrimination.* New York: Basic, 1978.

Goodman, Paul. *Growing Up Absurd.* New York: Vintage, 1960.

Gordon, Michael. "Cracking the Whip." *New York Times,* January 27, 1991.

Gottfried, Paul, and Thomas Fleming. *The Conservative Movement.* Boston: Twayne, 1988.

Hacker, Andrew. *Two Nations: Black and White, Separate, Hostile, Unequal.* New York: Ballantine, 1992.

Hammond, John Y. "Yuppies." *Public Opinion Quarterly,* 1986.

Harrington, Michael. *The Long Distance Runner: An Autobiography.* New York: Holt, 1988.

Harris, Fred, and Tom Wicker, eds. *The Kerner Report: The 1968 Report of the National Advisory Commission on Civil Disorders.* New York: Pantheon, 1988.

Hartz, Louis. *The Liberal Tradition in America.* New York: Harcourt, Brace and World, 1955.

Hayden, Casey, and Mary King. "A Kind of Memo." *Liberation,* April 1966.

Hayden, Tom. *Reunion: A Memoir.* New York: Pantheon, 1988.

Heinemann, Kenneth J. *Campus Wars: The Peace Movement at American State Universities in the Vietnam Era.* New York: New York University Press, 1993.

Hilliard, David. *This Side of Glory: The Autobiography of David Hilliard and the Story of the Black Panther Party.* Boston: Little, Brown, 1993.

Himmelstein, Jerome L. *To the Right: The Transformation of American Conservatism.* Berkeley: University of California Press, 1990.

Hobsbawm, Eric. *The Age of Extremes: A History of the World, 1914–1991* (esp. chaps. 10–16). New York: Pantheon, 1994.

Hodgson, Godfrey. *America in Our Time: From World War II to Nixon—What Happened and Why.* New York: Vintage, 1976.

Hoeveler, J. David, Jr. *Watch on the Right: Conservative Intellectuals in the Reagan Era.* Madison: University of Wisconsin Press, 1991.

hooks, bell. *Ain't I a Woman.* Boston: South End, 1981.

Horne, A. D., ed. *The Wounded Generation: After Vietnam.* Englewood Cliffs, N.J.: Prentice-Hall, 1981.

Hughes, Robert. *Culture of Complaint.* New York: Oxford University Press, 1993.

Isserman, Maurice. *If I Had a Hammer . . . The Death of the Old Left and the Birth of the New Left.* New York: Basic, 1987.

———. "The Not So Dark and Bloody Ground: New Works on the 1960s." *American Historical Review* 94 (October 1989): 990–1010.

Jackson, Kenneth T. *Crabgrass Frontier: The Suburbanization of the United States.* New York: Oxford University Press, 1985.

Jacoby, Russell. *Dogmatic Wisdom.* New York: Doubleday, 1994.

Jamison, Andrew, and Ron Eyerman. *Seeds of the Sixties.* Berkeley: University of California Press, 1994.

Jencks, Christopher. *Rethinking Social Policy*. New York: Harper, 1993.

Jezer, Marty. *The Dark Ages*. Boston: South End, 1982.

Johnson, Joyce. *Minor Characters*. New York: Pocket Books, 1984.

Jones, Jacqueline. *Labor of Love, Labor of Sorrow: Black Women, Work, and the Family from Slavery to the Present*. New York: Vintage, 1985.

Jones, LeRoi (Amiri Baraka). *Dutchman and The Slave: Two Plays*. New York: Morrow, 1964.

Journalist M. *A Year is Eight Months: Czechoslovakia, 1968*. New York: Anchor Doubleday, 1971.

Judis, John B. "Mister Ed." *New Republic*, April 27, 1987.

————. *William F. Buckley, Jr.: Patron Saint of the Conservatives*. New York: Simon & Schuster, 1988.

Kaminer, Wendy. *A Fearful Freedom: Women's Flight from Equality*. Reading, Mass.: Addison-Wesley, 1990.

————. "Feminism's Identity Crisis." *Atlantic Monthly*, October 1993.

Keniston, Kenneth. *The Uncommitted: Alienated Youth in American Society*. New York: Harcourt, Brace and World, 1965.

————. *Young Radicals: Notes on Committed Youth*. New York: Harcourt, Brace and World, 1968.

King, Mary. *Freedom Song: A Personal Story of the 1960s Civil Rights Movement*. New York: Morrow, 1987.

King, Richard. *The Party of Eros: Radical Social Thought and the Realm of Freedom*. Chapel Hill: University of North Carolina Press, 1972.

Kirkpatrick, Jeane J. *Dictatorships and Double Standards*. New York: Simon & Schuster, 1982.

Kotz, Nick, and Mary Lynn Kotz. *A Passion for Equality: George Wiley and the Movement*. New York: Norton, 1977.

Lasch, Christopher. *The New Radicalism in America*. New York: Vintage, 1965.

Lemann, Nicholas. *The Promised Land: The Great Black Migration and How It Changed America*. New York: Knopf, 1991.

Leuchtenburg, William E. *Franklin D. Roosevelt and the New Deal.* New York: Harper, 1963.

Levy, Frank. *Dollars and Dreams: The Changing American Income Distribution.* New York: Russell Sage Foundation, 1987.

Levy, Peter B. *The New Left and Labor in the 1960s.* Urbana: University of Illinois Press, 1994.

Lippmann, Walter. *The Cold War.* New York: Macmillan, 1947.

———. *Drift and Mastery.* Englewood Cliffs, N.J.: Prentice-Hall, 1961.

Lowenthal, Leo. *Literature, Popular Culture, and Society.* Palo Alto, Calif.: Pacific, 1968.

Luker, Kristin. *Abortion and the Politics of Motherhood.* Berkeley: University of California Press, 1984.

Lyons, Paul. *Class of '66: Living in Suburban Middle America.* Philadelphia: Temple University Press, 1994.

———. "Peggy Noonan: Conservative Baby Boomer." *Socialist Review,* January/March 1992.

MacKinnon, Catherine. *Feminism Unmodified.* Cambridge: Harvard University Press, 1987.

MacPherson, Myra. *Long Time Passing.* New York: Signet, 1984.

Maddox, William S., and Stuart A. Lillie. *Beyond Liberal and Conservative.* Washington, D.C.: Cato Institute, 1984.

Magnet, Myron. *The Dream and the Nightmare: The Sixties' Legacy to the Underclass.* New York: Morrow, 1993.

Mailer, Norman. *The Armies of the Night.* New York: New American Library, 1968.

———. *Miami and the Seige of Chicago.* New York: New American Library, 1968.

———. *Advertisements for Myself.* New York: Putnam, 1959.

———. *Of a Fire on the Moon.* New York: Signet, 1970.

———. *The Presidential Papers.* London: Andre Deutsch, 1964.

Mandle, Jay. *Not Slave, Not Free: The African-American Experience Since the Civil War.* Durham, N.C.: Duke University Press, 1992.

Mansbridge, Jane. *Why We Lost the ERA.* Chicago: University of Chicago Press, 1980.

Maraniss, David. *First in His Class: A Biography of Bill Clinton.* New York: Simon & Schuster, 1995.

Marcus, Greil. *Mystery Train.* New York: Dutton, 1976.

Marris, Peter, and Martin Rein. *Dilemmas of Social Reform.* New York: Atheneum, 1969.

Massey, Douglas S., and Nancy A. Denton. *American Apartheid: Segregation and the Making of the Underclass.* Cambridge: Harvard University Press, 1993.

Massing, Michael. "The Two Bill Bennetts." *New York Review of Books,* March 1, 1990.

May, Elaine Tyler. *Homeward Bound: American Families in the Cold War Era.* New York: Basic, 1988.

Mayer, William G. *The Changing American Mind.* Ann Arbor: University of Michigan Press, 1992.

Miles, Michael W. *The Odyssey of the American Right.* New York: Oxford University Press, 1980.

Miller, James. *"Democracy in the Streets": From Port Huron to the Siege of Chicago.* New York: Simon & Schuster, 1987.

Moore, Stanley. "Utopian Themes in Marx and Mao." *Dissent,* March/April 1970: 170–176.

Morgan, Edward P. *The 60s Experience: Hard Lessons about Modern America.* Philadelphia: Temple University Press, 1991.

Morgan, Robin, ed. *Sisterhood Is Powerful.* New York: Random House, 1970.

Moynihan, Daniel Patrick. *The Politics of a Guaranteed Income: The Nixon Administration and the Family Assistance Plan.* New York: Vintage, 1973.

Mueller, John. *War, Presidents, and Public Opinion.* New York: Wiley, 1973.

Murray, Charles. *Losing Ground.* New York: Basic, 1984.

National Advisory Commission on Civil Disorders. *Report of the National Commission on Civil Disorders.* New York: 1968

Noonan, Peggy. *What I Saw at the Revolution.* New York: Random House, 1990.

Office of the Secretary of Defense. "U.S. Military Personnel Who Died . . . in the Vietnam War, 1957–1986." Reprint from "Combat Area Casualties, 1957–1986." Record Group 330, National Archives.

O'Neill, William L. *Coming Apart: An Informal History of America in the 1960s.* New York: Quadrangle, 1971.

Patai, Daphne, and Noretta Koertge. *Professing Feminism: Cautionary Tales from the Strange World of Women's Studies.* New York: Basic, 1994.

Pearson, Hugh. *The Shadow of the Panther: Huey Newton and the Price of Black Power.* Reading, Mass.: Addison-Wesley, 1994.

Potter, David. *People of Plenty: Abundance and the American Character.* Chicago: University of Chicago Press, 1958.

Quadragno, Jill. *The Color of Welfare.* New York: Oxford University Press, 1994.

Rader, Dotson. *I Ain't Marchin' Anymore.* New York: Paperback Library, 1969.

Rainwater, Lee, and William L. Yancey. *The Moynihan Report and the Politics of Controversy.* Cambridge: MIT Press, 1967.

Ravitch, Diane. *The Troubled Crusade: American Education, 1945–1980.* New York: Basic, 1983.

Remnick, David. "Why Is Lee Atwater Happy?" *Esquire,* December 1986.

Roberts, James C. *The Conservative Decade: Emerging Leaders of the 1980s.* Westport, Conn.: Arlington House, 1980.

Rogin, Michael Paul. *The Intellectuals and McCarthy: The Radical Specter.* Boston: MIT Press, 1967.

Roiphe, Katie. *The Morning After.* Boston: Little, Brown, 1993.

Rorabaugh, W. J. *Berkeley at War: The 1960s.* New York: Oxford University Press, 1989.

Ryan, William. *Blaming the Victim.* New York: Pantheon, 1971.

Sack, Kevin, "Campaign Profile (William Kristol)." *New York Times,* September 1992.

Sale, Kirkpatrick. *The Green Revolution: The American Environmental Movement, 1962–1992.* New York: Hill & Wang, 1993.

————. *SDS*. New York: Random House, 1973.

Sayres, Sohnya, Anders Stephanson, Stanley Aronowitz, and Frederic Jameson, eds. *The 60s without Apology*. Minneapolis: University of Minnesota Press, 1984.

Schneider, William. "The Dawn of the Suburban Era in American Politics." *Atlantic*, July 1992: 33–44.

Sidel, Ruth. *Women and Children Last*. New York: Penguin, 1987.

Silver, James. *Mississippi: The Closed Society*. New York: Harcourt, Brace and World, 1963.

Silverman, Bertram, ed. *Man and Socialism in Cuba*. New York: Atheneum, 1971.

Sklar, Martin J. *The United States as a Developing Country: Studies in U.S. History in the Progressive Era and the 1920s*. Cambridge: Cambridge University Press, 1992.

Sleeper, Jim. *The Closest of Strangers: Liberalism and the Politics of Race in New York*. New York: Norton, 1990.

Sniderman, Paul M., and Thomas Piazza. *The Scar of Race*. Cambridge: Harvard University Press, Belknap Press, 1993.

Sommers, Christina Hoff. *Who Stole Feminism?* New York: Simon & Schuster, 1994.

Stampp, Kenneth M. *The Peculiar Institution: Slavery in the Antebellum South*. New York: Knopf, 1956.

Stan, Adele. *Debating Sexual Correctness*. New York: Delta, 1995.

Steele, Shelby. *The Content of Our Character*. New York: St. Martin's, 1990.

Steinfels, Peter. *The Neo-Conservatives*. New York: Touchstone, 1980.

Stiegerwald, David. *The Sixties and the End of Modern America*. New York: St. Martin's, 1995.

Stockman, David. *The Triumph of Politics*. New York: Harper & Row, 1986.

Susman, Warren I. *Culture and History: The Transformation of American Society in the Twentieth Century*. New York: Pantheon, 1984.

Tavris, Carol. *Mismeasure of Woman*. New York: Simon & Schuster, 1992.

Teachout, Terry, ed. *Beyond the Boom: New Voices on American Life, Culture, and Politics*. New York: Poseidon, 1990.

Thorne, Melvin J. *American Conservative Thought Since World War II*. Westport, Conn.: Greenwood, 1990.

Tischler, Barbara, ed. *Sights on the Sixties*. New Brunswick: Rutgers University Press, 1992.

Trilling, Lionel. *The Liberal Imagination*. New York: Anchor Doubleday, 1954.

Wakefield, Dan. *New York in the Fifties*. Boston: Houghton Mifflin, 1992.

Wattenberg, Benjamin J., and Richard Scammon. *The Real Majority*. New York: Coward-McCann, 1970.

Webb, James. *A Country Such As This*. New York: Bantam, 1985.

————. *Fields of Fire*. Englewood Cliffs, N.J.: Prentice-Hall, 1978.

Weber, Max. *The Theory of Social and Economic Organization*. New York: Free Press, 1964.

Wells, Tom. *The War Within: America's Battle over Vietnam*. Berkeley: University of California Press, 1994.

Wheeler, John. *Touched with Fire*. New York: Avon, 1984.

Williams, Raymond. *Keywords*. New York: Oxford University Press, 1976.

Williams, William A. *The Tragedy of American Diplomacy*. New York: Dell/Delta Books, 1972.

Wills, Ellen. *No More Nice Girls: Countercultural Essays*. Hanover, N.H.: University Press of New England and Wesleyan University Press, 1992.

Wills, Garry. *The Kennedy Imprisonment*. Boston: Little, Brown, 1981.

Wilson, William Julius. *The Declining Significance of Race: Blacks and Changing American Institutions*. Chicago: University of Chicago Press, 1980.

————. *The Truly Disadvantaged: The Inner City, the Underclass, and Public Policy*. Chicago: University of Chicago Press, 1987.

Wolf, Naomi. *The Beauty Myth*. New York: Morrow, 1991.

————. *Fire with Fire*. New York: Random House, 1993.

Wolfe, Alan. *America's Impasse: The Rise and Fall of the Politics of Growth*. New York: Pantheon, 1981.

————. "The Good, the Bad, and Gingrich." *New Republic,* May 1, 1995: 35–41.

Wolfe, Tom. *The Bonfire of the Vanities*. New York: Bantam, 1988.

————. *The Purple Decades: A Reader*. New York: Berkeley, 1987.

————. *Radical Chic and Mau-Mauing the Flak Catchers*. New York: Bantam, 1971.

Wyatt, David. *Out of the Sixties: Storytelling and the Vietnam Generation*. Cambridge: Cambridge University Press, 1993.

Yankelovich, Daniel. *New Rules*. New York: Bantam, 1982.

Zaroulis, Nancy, and Gerald Sullivan. *Who Spoke Up?* Garden City, N.Y.: Doubleday, 1984.

Index